P9-EDP-469

Ex Libris
Universitatis
Albertensis

THE MUSIC OF HARRY FREEDMAN

Harry Freedman. Photo by André Leduc.

GAIL DIXON

The Music of Harry Freedman

UNIVERSITY OF TORONTO PRESS
Toronto Buffalo London

© University of Toronto Press Incorporated 2004
Toronto Buffalo London
Printed in Canada

ISBN 0-8020-8964-X

Printed on acid-free paper

National Library of Canada Cataloguing in Publication

Dixon, Gail Susan, 1936–
   Music of Harry Freedman / Gail Dixon.

   Includes bibliographical references and index.
   ISBN 0-8020-8964-X

   1. Freedman, Harry, 1922–   2. Freedman, Harry, 1922– – Criticism
   and interpretation.   I. Title.

   ML410.F853D62 2004   780'.92   C2004-901303-3

University of Toronto Press acknowledges the financial assistance to its
publishing program of the Canada Council for the Arts and the Ontario
Arts Council.

This book has been published with the help of a grant from the Canadian
Federation for the Humanities and Social Sciences, through the Aid to
Scholarly Publications Programme, using funds provided by the Social
Sciences and Humanities Research Council of Canada.

University of Toronto Press acknowledges the financial support for its
publishing activities of the Government of Canada through the Book
Publishing Industry Development Program (BPIDP).

AUGUSTANA LIBRARY
UNIVERSITY OF ALBERTA

Contents

Acknowledgments

I have derived great pleasure from writing this book, not only because of the many riches I have uncovered in Harry Freedman's music, but also because of the insights I have gained in conversation with Freedman himself. He has graciously made himself available on countless occasions to answer my questions and provide information. These encounters, too numerous to document, extend over a period of several decades, and include telephone conversations, e-mail correspondence, and interviews. He has provided not only factual information about his works but also illuminating details about his compositional methods. I am also grateful to him for granting permission to publish excerpts from his sketches and scores.

Numerous other people have also proved very helpful. I wish to acknowledge the indulgence of the Canadian Music Centre in making available to me for extended periods of time literally hundreds of scores, tapes, and other materials. I am also indebted to many of my colleagues who have generously offered their advice and encouragement throughout this project. In particular, I wish to thank my husband, Michael, for his invaluable assistance in preparing the musical examples that are such an important component of this book.

Permissions

Excerpts from his scores and sketches are reprinted by permission of Harry Freedman.

Excerpts from *Images* are reprinted by permission of Berandol Music Limited.

Excerpts from *Tableau* are reprinted by permission of the publisher G. Ricordi & Co. (Canada) Ltd., and their agent, Counterpoint Musical Services.

Keewaydin, by Harry Freedman. © 1972 (Renewed) Gordon V. Thompson, Ltd. All rights reserved. Used by permission. Warner Bros. Publications U.S. Inc., Miami, FL. 33014.

THE MUSIC OF HARRY FREEDMAN

Chapter One
Introduction

In a seminal article written in 1969, Canadian composer and scholar John Beckwith deplored the lack of recognition accorded the music of Canadian composers, not only within Canada but also in the international musical community: 'the reluctance to give recognition to the prime rôle played by composers in our musical life is virtually total.'[1] This bleak assessment was echoed eleven years later by George Proctor, when he described the continuing plight of Canadian music: 'Canadian concert music ... has yet to receive the depth of understanding and informed appreciation which it deserves.'[2]

In the intervening years, the situation has been ameliorated by a steady and substantial outpouring of research on music and musicians in Canada, research whose crowning achievement was, arguably, the monumental and comprehensive *Encyclopedia of Music in Canada*,[3] currently in its second edition. Now that much of the essential groundwork has been laid, scholars have ready access to the overview and perspective that are invaluable adjuncts to the more narrowly focused research necessary in monographs. Only a small number of Canadian composers have as yet been the subject of book-length studies.[4] The monographs that have already been published have filled an obvious need, and have fuelled a demand for further such studies. High on the list of composers whose music merits detailed investigation is Harry Freedman.

Harry Freedman has been an important and respected figure on the Canadian music scene for over half a century. His output as a composer has been both prodigious and eclectic. Extraordinarily prolific, he has created over one hundred and seventy-five works in a wide variety of genres including symphonies, concertos, string quartets, operas, ballets, film scores, popular songs, and jazz pieces. His style ranges from the austerely twelve-tone to the audaciously aleatoric, from the self-consciously 'square' to the unabashedly 'cool.' The inspirations for his compositions are as varied as the compositions themselves, and include painting, literature, mathematics, philosophy, jazz, and folk music.

Widely respected in the Canadian musical world, Freedman is the recipient of numerous awards and honours, including being named Composer of the Year in 1979 by the Canadian Music Council and an Officer of the Order of Canada in 1984. His works have been discussed in the general musical literature as comprehensively as have those of any other major Canadian composer. However, apart from three theses, each of which allocates a substantial number of pages to Freedman, and several articles devoted exclusively to his works,[5] there has been little focused research. Regrettably, our understanding of the details of Freedman's style and development remains fragmentary at best. For example, how did he navigate the winding path from the modest neoclassical pieces of his early years to the broadly eclectic works of his mature period? Are there style characteristics that transcend changes in period and genre? To which musical traditions and figures from the past does he acknowledge a debt? What roles do literature, the visual arts, and other extramusical disciplines play in his work? How does he go about composing a work, and what are the relationships between his compositional sketches and his finished scores? These and many other questions will be addressed in the coming pages.

My aim in writing this book has been not simply to raise awareness of Freedman's music in the minds of the general public and to make it more accessible, but also to investigate it, in and of itself, with a view to illuminating its underlying principles, stylistic development, and means of coherence. The book is designed primarily as a study of his music, and only secondarily as a biography. His works will be dealt with chronologically and illuminated, where relevant, with biographical detail. To avoid the spectre of superficiality that would inevitably beset any attempt to discuss Freedman's enormous output in its entirety, certain works have been selected for detailed analysis. The chronological presentation of these works will facilitate a clear understanding of Freedman's compositional style in its dramatic evolution from the tentative serial explorations of his early works to the eclectic stylistic spectrum of his mature works. Periodic summaries will illustrate that despite the obvious changes in his style it is possible to isolate certain enduring characteristics and procedures. An essential adjunct to the text are the nearly one hundred musical examples, some of which have been reproduced directly from Freedman's own autograph scores.

In order to build a coherent picture of Freedman's stylistic evolution, the examination of his oeuvre must necessarily extend over a broad range of musical parameters. From a practical perspective this goal is best achieved by focusing on a limited number of parameters in any given work. Several criteria have been used in selecting compositions to be discussed. A work may be included because it constitutes an important evolutionary link in Freedman's stylistic development, or because it is representative of his style at a particular point in time. On the other hand, a composition may be singled out for detailed study simply because it is unusual, or is widely viewed as particularly important in his oeuvre. The application of these criteria to the choice of works from his earliest years results in the inclusion of almost all of them, because his style at that stage was evolving so rapidly. As his works become more numerous, a smaller proportion is selected for analysis. In the face of the enormous output of the years following 1977 it has inevitably been necessary to omit a number of important and otherwise entirely worthy compositions in favour of a judicious selection from among them.

Several common analytic conventions have been used in this book. Register is specified by superscript numbers, where C^1 ... B^1 represents the lowest octave above the bottom C on the piano. Traditional pitch nomenclature such as $C^\#$, A^b, D^x is used when reference is made to specific pitches in a score. In other cases integers are used to represent pitch, as follows: C=0, $C^\#/D^b$=1 ... $A^\#/B^b$=10, B=11. Of the several different methods of labelling row forms in serial music I have chosen the following: the prime form of the row is rendered in integer notation and assigned the label P0 at its original pitch level. The labels P1, P2 ... P11 denote the prime form transposed up by one, two ... eleven semitones respectively. The retrograde of the prime form at its original pitch level is labelled RP0. RP1, RP2 ... RP11 denote the retrograde of the prime form transposed up by one, two ... eleven semitones. Similarly, I0 refers to the inversion of P0, RI0 to the retrograde of I0.

Examples:

P0:	5	3	6	2	1	0	7	11	4	10	9	8
RP0:	8	9	10	4	11	7	0	1	2	6	3	5
P2:	7	5	8	4	3	2	9	1	6	0	11	10
RP2:	10	11	0	6	1	9	2	3	4	8	5	7
I0:	5	7	4	8	9	10	3	11	6	0	1	2
RI0:	2	1	0	6	11	3	10	9	8	4	7	5
I2:	7	9	6	10	11	0	5	1	8	2	3	4

I have made the assumption that the reader has some grasp of other fundamental analytic terms and techniques normally associated with the twentieth-century repertoire. In particular, some of the tools of pitch class set theory have proven useful in illuminating aspects of Freedman's music. However, a lack of analytic expertise in this area should not deter the prospective reader. The following brief explanation will provide sufficient information about pitch class sets to allow the uninitiated to follow most of the analyses.

The term 'pitch' is normally restricted to a specific tone in a specific register, as in A^3, or D^5, while the term 'pitch class' (abbreviated as pc) is non-specific as to register, A^n or D^n in this instance. Two pitch classes (pcs) separated by a semitone or its octave multiple (e.g., C^n to $C^{\# n}$/ $D^{b n}$), or its inversion, eleven semitones or octave multiple (e.g., $C^{\# n}$/ $D^{b n}$ to C^n), are said to be a representation of interval class 1, or ic1. Similarly, two pcs separated by two or ten, three or nine, four or eight, five or seven, or six semitones or their octave multiples are said to be representations of ic2, ic3, ic4, ic5, and ic6, respectively.

In my analyses, certain collections of notes are isolated from their surroundings and identified by labels such as pc set class 6-2 (012346) or 3-3 (014). These labels are drawn from tables containing all intervallically unique collections of from three to nine elements.[6] The first figure in each case refers to the number of elements in the collection, the second figure to the number assigned to that class of pc sets in the table, and the figures in parentheses to its intervallic components. For example, the four tones of pc set class 4-5 (0126) consist of an original tone along with three others, one, two, and six semitones higher or lower. When translated into actual musical tones those elements could be, for example, C, $C^\#$/D^b, D, $F^\#$/G^b or their inversion. Transposition level is abbreviated as t=n semitones, so that the pitch classes shown above at t=4 would become E, F, $F^\#$/G^b, $A^\#$/B^b. A pc set class whose intervallic contents can be found within a larger one is referred to as a subset. For example, pc set class 3-5 (016) is a subset of pc set class 4-5 (0126). Pc set class 3-4 (015) is another subset of pc set class 4-5 (0126) in that the elements of pc set 3-4 at t=1 replicate intervallically the last three elements of pc set class 4-5. Similarly, pc set class 4-5 is a superset of both pc set classes 3-4 and 3-5. Any other potentially obscure terms or concepts will be described in the endnotes immediately following their initial use.

I shall be discussing more than fifty of Freedman's works, some of which may not be easily available to the reader. To address this problem, I have included in the body of the text a substantial number of musical excerpts.[7] Specific places in the scores or excerpts are referred to by rehearsal letters or numbers followed by figures which indicate the number of measures before or after a rehearsal number or letter. For example, 'Rehearsal C+4' refers to the fourth measure after rehearsal letter C, while 'Rehearsal 2–7' specifies the seventh measure before rehearsal number 2. Note that the measure that begins at Rehearsal A, for example, is Rehearsal A+1, not Rehearsal A+0. Measure numbers refer to the first full measure of an excerpt, excluding anacruses.

Freedman occasionally revises his works, often many years after they have been written. His revisions are rarely sweeping, sometimes amounting to little more than small emendations, substitutions, or additions. However, when he revises a work he withdraws the original from circulation, thus creating a dilemma for the analyst. It would clearly be impracticable to introduce such a work using the original version of the score, since it is not readily available. On the other hand, it would be misleading to defer presentation of the work until the period in which the revisions were actually done, because the main ideas and basic structure of the work are the products of an earlier period of Freedman's development. Instead, I intend a compromise: I shall present the work in the period in which it was first composed, but I shall use the revised score, being careful not to select for detailed analysis any portion of that work which was later substantially revised.

In writing a monograph on a creative personality such as Freedman it is usually considered desirable to provide a balance between favourable and unfavourable comments in order to achieve an honest report. I have certainly not shrunk from criticizing certain works, when in my view such criticism is justified. However, the amount of time spent in the close analysis of so many scores would hardly have been worthwhile were it not for my conviction of their generally high quality. It should also be said that this book represents my own perspective on Freedman's music, and should be read as such. Although I have consulted with the composer frequently on a number of issues, he is not in any way responsible for any errors in judgment or fact that may appear.

Chapter Two

The Early Years (to 1952)

Harry Freedman was born on 5 April 1922 in Lodz, Poland. The family immigrated in 1925 to Medicine Hat, Alberta, where they spent six years before settling permanently in Winnipeg in 1931.[1] Freedman remembers his father only as a shadowy, almost completely emasculated figure in a household entirely dominated by his mother. This highly artistic and accomplished woman had been a nurse and governess for a wealthy family in Berlin before the First World War. She sang quite well, spoke several languages, and was proficient in drawing and crafts. It is not surprising that it was she who provided the artistic encouragement so vital to the young Freedman. Aggressive and ambitious, she saw to it that Harry, along with his older brother and younger sister, adopted pursuits that brought them into contact with interesting, cultured, and talented people.

Freedman soon developed a keen interest in the visual arts, and at the age of fourteen he enrolled in classes at the Winnipeg School of Art.[2] At the same time, he was attending St John's High School in Winnipeg, where he was staff artist on the school newspaper. In an interview with Helmut Blume, Freedman recalls some of his experiences in those early years:

In fact, in my teens I had no musical aspirations. I was studying at the Winnipeg School of Art whose principal at that time was the late LeMoine Fitzgerald. During this period I was developing an interest in music: jazz exclusively at first, then gradually, through the usual Nutcracker, Unfinished, Valse Triste cycle, an ever-widening interest in 'serious' music. It was during this period that the similarity between music and painting first occurred to me. I remember being obsessed with the idea of a series of paintings presenting my visual impressions of the styles of several composers and jazz musicians. Then as my interest in music grew this changed to another idea, that of composing music based on the styles of famous painters, or paintings. I still recall how bitterly disappointed I was when in the course of my expanding knowledge of music I discovered that Moussorgsky had already done something along these lines in his 'Pictures at an Exhibition'. In any case, it was these early interests – jazz and painting – that I still recognize as the predominant influences in my attitude to music.[3]

Despite his lack of formal musical training in his youth, Freedman did obtain some valuable musical experience during his high school years when he sang one of the lead roles in the school production of Gilbert and Sullivan's *The Gondoliers*. In 1938 he graduated from high school with honours, but despite his exceptional ability in mathematics he refused a scholarship to pursue this interest at university. Nor did he elect to continue his studies at the Winnipeg School of Art. Freedman speculates that his mother's strong ambition to have her son succeed in the visual arts field might instead have inspired in him a kind of adolescent rebellion. In any case, he became intensely interested in music, and began studying clarinet while working part-time to finance his studies. He was employed first in a drug store and later in a movie theatre, where he absorbed involuntarily much information that was later to be useful to him in writing film scores. He studied music on and off for six years, during which time he played with and wrote for various dance bands and jazz groups in Winnipeg. In a remarkably short time he obtained his first professional job, as clarinettist with a dance band. His clarinet teacher, Arthur Hart, also encouraged him to buy pocket scores of the great classics of the orchestral literature, copy out the clarinet parts, and play along with the recordings.

Freedman was fortunate at this time to have come in contact with a bandmaster, Captain J.F. O'Donnell, who taught him the traditional subjects of harmony and counterpoint in an unusually creative and non-pedantic manner, with a strong compositional bias. Concurrently with the absorption of this formal material, Freedman was listening avidly to the music of the 'big bands' of Count Basie and Duke Ellington on the radio. Clearly, the young musician's taste was being shaped in these formative years by a broad variety of styles.

In 1942 he joined the Royal Canadian Air Force and played first clarinet with the famed Central Silver Band. His extensive travels throughout Canada with this and other bands left him with a lasting impression of the vastness, beauty, and essential loneliness of the country, an impression that was later to be reflected in some of his compositions. During this period he bought an oboe and began teaching himself to play it, because he thought that the Winnipeg Symphony Orchestra might soon be in a position to hire an oboist. He also began writing 'charts,' or arrangements, for the band. Toward the end of the war, he became a member of a group that went to the Arctic to entertain the troops. In addition to functioning as performer and arranger for the group, Freedman confides that he was its stand-up comedian. Reposted to Winnipeg, he joined a band in which he could play the oboe rather than the clarinet. Certainly Freedman's wartime experiences could not be described as musically unproductive. Indeed, he recalls with pleasure, and not a little nostalgia, the unusually cultivated men who were his closest companions during those years.

After the war he was given a rehabilitation grant which covered four years of study plus a living allowance. The timing was opportune because, at twenty-three years of age, he recognized that further formal musical training had become a matter of urgent necessity for him. With typical energy, he plunged into oboe lessons with Perry Bauman, piano lessons with Margaret Butler, and composition lessons with John Weinzweig, all at the Toronto Conservatory of Music (now the Royal Conservatory of Music). In the lessons with Weinzweig, which continued until 1951, he worked through Hindemith's *A Concentrated Course in Traditional Harmony* and analysed many scores, in particular those of Webern, Berg, Stravinsky, Bartók, and Bach. Freedman claims that two of the most important lessons he learned from Weinzweig were how to find out for himself what he wished to know and how to be self-critical. Under Weinzweig's tutelage, Freedman was soon composing sizeable pieces, mostly in a highly chromatic, neoclassical style.

In 1946, Sir Ernest MacMillan and Ettore Mazzoleni auditioned Freedman for a position as English horn player with the Toronto Symphony Orchestra. He actually had to borrow an instrument from his teacher for the occasion. Though his auditioners realized that his technique on the instrument was still imperfect, they made the assumption, later proved to be correct, that Freedman's skill would soon match the demands of the position. For the next twenty-four years he successfully juggled two careers, one as a full-time orchestral player, the other as a remarkably prolific composer.

The *Divertimento for Oboe and Strings* was written in 1947 after Freedman had completed his preliminary studies in traditional harmony, counterpoint, and analysis. This was his first attempt at composition, other than writing 'charts' for dance bands or assignments for his composition lessons with Weinzweig. Like many of Freedman's early works, the style of his *Divertimento* could be characterized as neoclassical. Ten minutes in duration, it comprises three formally conventional movements marked 'Allegretto,' 'Slow,' and 'Lively and rhythmic,' respectively. The music is dissonant, contrapuntal, and motivic. Recurrence of material at some level of transposition is a frequent means of obtaining coherence. Although focal pitches can be found in abundance, particularly in the first movement, the writing is not tonal in the traditional sense.

The very first melodic gesture of the work incorporates the intervallic content of the motive that was to become one of his trademarks: that is, a representation of pc set class 3-5 (016) realized as a rising perfect fourth followed by a rising minor second. However, the characteristic shape of that trademark motive is missing here. Not only is the contour inverted, but the opening pitch F serves only a subsidiary function with respect to the following pitches E and B.[4] In fact, E is the tonal focus not only of the opening phrases (see example 2-1) but also of the entire first movement.

Example 2-1: *Divertimento for Oboe and Strings*, Movement I, measures 1 to 10

Several authors have commented on the resemblance between Freedman's *Divertimento* and that of his teacher, John Weinzweig, written in the previous year. According to Elaine Keillor, author of a full-length study on Weinzweig, this work (his *Divertimento no. 1* for flute and orchestra) 'exemplifies basic characteristics of Weinzweig's mature style. The relationship between the solo flute and the accompanying strings is based on the concept of dialogue, using certain rhythmic figures and melodic ideas. ... Generally the contrapuntal writing is non-imitative, but a few touches of imitation appear to create more cohesion and interplay between flute and orchestra.'[5] The characteristics she describes are very much in evidence in Freedman's *Divertimento* as well. In fact, one wonders whether the resemblance extends beyond a sharing of general stylistic traits. The opening trichords of the first and second movements of the Weinzweig work are also representations of pc set class 3-5, in an ascending shape in the first movement and descending in the second. Compare these with the bracketed trichords in the Freedman work, as shown in example 2-1.

In 1948 Freedman composed two important works, *Symphonic Suite* and a theme and variations on the theme 'Just a Poor Wayfarin' Stranger.' He was particularly pleased with the recognition given his *Symphonic Suite*, a fourteen-minute piece for full orchestra, since it was chosen to be played at a symposium of music students from prestigious institutions such as the University of Toronto, the Juilliard School of Music, the Curtis Institute, and Yale University's School of Music. Freedman claims that the *Symphonic Suite* was the locus of his first experiment with the 'twelve-tone technique,' as he called it at that time, though what he meant was obviously not the more contemporary connotation of the term as an analogue for serialism, but rather a deliberately egalitarian use of all twelve tones. The work is in three movements, and is stylistically akin to the type of neoclassicism exhibited in contemporaneous works like Barbara Pentland's *String Quartet no. 1*. Formally based on traditional models, the *Symphonic Suite* relies considerably on immediate repetition and subsequent recurrence of material as important means of obtaining coherence. The work is contrapuntal, but not particularly imitative, with pedals and ostinati as occasional features of the texture. There is a limited number of motives, and these are manipulated in traditional ways such as intervallic modification, inversion, fragmentation, and ornamentation. Motives that are introduced singly occasionally recur superposed, and there is a loose family resemblance between some of the materials, both within and between movements.

Despite Freedman's putative goal of achieving an equitable distribution of the twelve tones, focal pitches do emerge at critical formal junctures, particularly at the beginnings and endings of movements and at major internal articulation points. Chords, especially those in prominent positions, appear to be triadic in origin, though the third above the root is often coloured with an accessory tone (G, B♭, B♮, D, for example). Freedman also experiments with strings of parallel triads to support an independent melodic line.[6] Both the coexistence of several forms of third and parallelism in various guises were to become important features of Freedman's technical armament.

As well, there is an interesting experiment in ornamentation in the second movement. The three motives of the opening theme (labelled 'a,' 'b,' and 'c' in example 2-2.1) occur in reverse order when the thematic material recurs at Rehearsal D+1 (example 2-2.2). In addition, the constituent tones of each motive are rearranged. The last two measures of example 2-2.2 demonstrate a more conventional means of elaboration: the last measure elaborates its predecessor with melodic interpolations.

Example 2-2.1: *Symphonic Suite,* Movement II, Rehearsal A–5 to A–1, first flute only

Example 2-2.2: *Symphonic Suite,* Movement II, Rehearsal D+1 to D+7, first flute only

The piece is solidly crafted, though clearly it is still a student effort. There is an almost self-conscious reliance upon time-honoured techniques.

Stylistically even less adventurous than the *Symphonic Suite* is the *Trio for Two Oboes and English Horn,* a set of variations written in the same year. The conservative nature of the work may have been a response to the orthodox nature of the theme 'Just a Poor Wayfarin' Stranger,' which is in G Aeolian and cast in three eight-measure phrases (AAB). The variations adhere to the classical model, with each maintaining a unique character, melodic motive, and rhythm. The chordal introduction and opening eight measures of the theme are shown in example 2-3.[7]

Example 2-3: Theme from *Trio for Two Oboes and English Horn*, measures 1 to 14

This is the first in a long list of Freedman's works to include literal musical quotation. Here he paid homage to Debussy, whose scores he had studied extensively and greatly admired, by including a quotation from one of the *Trois Nocturnes*. In Variation 6 the two oboes reproduce the outer voices from the opening measures of 'Nuages,' while the English horn provides a contrasting contrapuntal line (example 2-4). The idea for including this particular quotation was obviously suggested by an insignificant four-note fragment, bracketed in example 2-3, within the 'Poor Wayfarin' Stranger' theme. Freedman moved this fragment to the beginning of the phrase, doubled its note values and changed its metrical placement. Coupled with the harmony produced by the other oboe, the reference to the Debussy's 'Nuages' is absolutely transparent.

In 1949 Freedman was given an opportunity to study at Tanglewood with two eminent composers, Olivier Messiaen and Aaron Copland. Each composer taught a class of eight composition students. Because Freedman came from Canada it was assumed that he spoke French,

Example 2-4: *Trio for Two Oboes and English Horn*, Variation 6, measures 1 to 4

so he was put in Messiaen's group. He did not speak French at the time, in fact, so found the classes somewhat difficult. Despite this problem, he did learn from Messiaen a new approach to rhythm through the application of analytic procedures based on East Indian rhythms. Oddly enough, Messiaen never attempted to impose upon the students his own idiosyncratic techniques, his non-retrogradable rhythms, or modes of limited transposition.

Periodically the two groups of students joined together for communal lectures taught by either Copland or Messiaen. While Freedman liked neither Messiaen's music nor his quasi-mystical approach to his art, he found in Copland a kindred spirit from whom he absorbed a great deal about the use of orchestral colour and the incorporation of jazz elements into serious composition. One of Copland's statements that left an indelible impression on Freedman was that music should be as simple as possible, but no simpler.

In the article on Freedman in *Thirty-Four Biographies of Canadian Composers*, he is quoted as stating that two movements of his *Five Pieces for String Quartet* (completed in 1949) were written using what he describes as 'twelve-tone technique.'[8] In contemporary usage the term is normally applied to serial music, but, as noted above, Freedman used it at that time to describe an equitable distribution of the tones in the chromatic scale. However, certain aspects of serialism are indeed present in the work, and in more than two of its movements, though the reader will search in vain for any comprehensive use of strict serial procedures. Freedman did not embrace full-blown serialism until later in his career.

Movement I of his *Five Pieces for String Quartet* contains three motivically interrelated themes, none of which contains all twelve tones.[9] In this movement extensive use is made of one of the techniques associated with serial practice, that is the appearance of a succession of tones in prime and retrograde forms along with their inversions. The first theme appears in all four of these forms, and at multiple levels of transposition. However, the sequence of intervals found in the theme is never dissociated from the original rhythmic shape of the theme. Despite the frequent extraction of short motives for independent use, the full series, if such it can be called, is restricted to thematic use. This movement, like most of the others, is a virtual compendium of contrapuntal techniques such as imitation (often canonic), fragmentation, recombination, and rhythmic augmentation and diminution. The final chord is a D major triad, though this is the only overtly tonal reference in the movement.

The theme of the second movement consists of twelve unique pitches, unfolded gradually with much internal repetition of previously heard segments. The numerals in example 2-5 are order numbers.

Example 2-5: *Five Pieces for String Quartet*, Movement II, from the beginning to Rehearsal A, first violin only

This sequence of twelve tones appears only in prime and inverted forms and, as in the first movement, it is never dissociated from its thematic context. However, order numbers 4 to 8 are verticalized in the opening chords of the movement.

Movement III introduces several more explicit references to serial technique. For the first time Freedman recasts a twelve-tone theme in new rhythmic and metrical contexts, thus specifically divesting the generative pitch material of its thematic associations. Note that the opening and closing trichords of the row are representations of pc set class 3-4 (015), a relationship that may have been deliberate on Freedman's part, since he uses that motive extensively throughout the movement (example 2-6).

The material following Rehearsal C provides several excellent examples of the extraction of a segment from the row for independent use. In example 2-7 the opening thematic material appears in parallel thirds between first and second violins while order numbers 9 to 12 from four

Example 2-6: *Five Pieces for String Quartet*, Movement III, measures 1 to 10

different transpositions of the row provide the material for the accompaniment.

Lest the foregoing examples suggest that similar orderly procedures are widespread throughout the work, it must be said that much of the writing cannot be traced to a generative pitch source. At most, *Five Pieces* can be said to manifest incipient serialism.

When compared with *Five Pieces*, *Nocturne* (also written in 1949) reveals increased subtlety and skill, both in the creation of a distinctive mood and in the incorporation of serial techniques. Freedman creates a mysterious and compelling aura right at the outset with the slow, undulating background of muted horns and harp supporting a haunting motive in parallel thirds in the winds and muted strings. He modifies this mood in subtle ways throughout the work, exhibiting a new sensitivity in the management of instrumental colour, dynamics, and texture. The work is far more strictly serial than any of its predecessors, though the row exists in two slightly different versions, with pitch class D being assigned a variable position. The principal version, consisting of pitch classes 11 0 9 4 8 1 5 2 7 3 10 6, is projected thematically

Example 2-7: *Five Pieces for String Quartet*, Movement III, Rehearsal C+5 to C+6

in the English horn at Rehearsal A (measure 11 of example 2-8).[10] Prior to the composition of *Nocturne*, Freedman had rarely used the contents of a single row statement to construct his simultaneities, preferring instead to superpose linear statements of different row forms. He now achieves a new kind of integration and coherence by deploying the pitch classes of a single row vertically as well as sequentially, as shown in example 2-8.

Although Freedman was reasonably faithful to the original row orderings in this work, he did not hesitate to deviate when it served his purposes to do so. Two instances are evident in example 2-8. The departure from row ordering in the clarinet and bassoon dyads in measures 5 to 9 clearly results from the composer's desire to echo the parallel thirds of the opening. The second instance occurs from measure 23 to measure 26 where the oboe and first flute parts feature an important fragment comprised of order numbers 10, 11, and 12 of P0. The selection of order numbers 10, 5, 2 (E^b, A^b, C) for sequential presentation in

Example 2-8: *Nocturne*, measures 1 to 26, woodwinds only

the clarinet and bassoon in measures 24 to 26 is likely to have been made in order to mirror the intervallic content of the original E♭, B♭, G♭ motive. Note that both trichords are representations of pc set class 3-11 (037).

The year 1951 was a particularly busy one for Freedman. During the period following the Second World War he and a number of other contemporary Canadian composers had become increasingly aware of the need for legitimacy within the Canadian cultural milieu. In order to counter a perceived public resistance to their music and to establish composition as a recognized profession in Canada, Freedman and a small group of like-minded individuals came together in 1951 to form the Canadian League of Composers. The group's first president was John Weinzweig, its first secretary, Harry Freedman. An active lobbyist within the group for many years, Freedman served as its president from 1975 to 1978.

In 1951 he married soprano Mary Morrison, an enthusiastic and sensitive performer of contemporary Canadian music. She taught Freedman much about the capabilities of the voice, particularly its capacity to be used instrumentally. Morrison's is the voice in a number of Freedman's film scores, and she premièred several of his works, including *Two Vocalises* (1954), *Toccata* (1968), and *Fragments of Alice* (1976).

Also in 1951 Freedman wrote the five-movement *Suite for Piano*. This is a collection of short pieces modelled on the Baroque suite. Each movement has its own distinct character, motive, rhythm, and texture, with all the essential elements of each movement clearly projected in its opening few measures. Freedman appears to have used the *Suite* as a venue for experimenting with new techniques, in particular those used by Bartók in his *Mikrokosmos*. Each movement focuses on specific devices: ostinati, octatonic scales, and parallel triads for one of the movements, for example, and changing metres and asymmetrical accents for another. There is no evidence of twelve-tone serialism in any of the movements, although Freedman frequently reveals his interest in the equality of all twelve tones by encompassing the aggregate within a short space of time.

Freedman's first foray into the realm of humour and parody comes with the composition of his *Matinée Suite*, composed between the years 1951 and 1955 for a radio show called 'Opportunity Knocks.' Like the *Suite for Piano*, the three pieces that make up the *Matinée Suite* manifest a marked affinity with the styles of certain early twentieth-century composers, notably Prokofiev and Copland. The first piece in the suite, 'Caricature' (1951), is reminiscent of some of Prokofiev's writing in his *Classical Symphony*. On the surface the music seems absolutely traditional. It is a march, with typical rhythms and off-beat accompaniment. The opening theme, set as a repeated symmetrical parallel period, incorporates a series of triadic outlines, and is accompanied by triadic chords. However, the presence of 'wrong' notes in the triadic outlines (for example, an arpeggiated E to G to B to E^b in the melody) and the lack of a common harmonic basis between the theme and its accompaniment quickly disabuse the listener of any notion that the piece might have been written in the eighteenth century. The second piece of the suite, 'March for Small Types' (1952), is very similar to 'Caricature,' though the accompaniment is more pungent, featuring an ostinato of parallel seconds and ninths. The last piece, 'Harlem Hoedown' (1955),[11] inevitably recalls elements of *Rodeo* by one of Freedman's mentors, Aaron Copland. Unlike other movements of this suite, this one has a key signature, and is clearly in D major throughout. Example 2-9 illustrates the 'oompah' accompaniment which this movement shares with portions of Copland's *Rodeo*, as well as the 'blues' third and seventh which were to become increasingly important elements in Freedman's writing.[12]

Example 2-9: 'Harlem Hoedown,' Rehearsal A+1 to Rehearsal A+6, piano and first violin

The year 1952 stands out as particularly important in Freedman's estimation, because with the composition of his *Tableau* for string orchestra he felt he had truly 'come of age' as a composer. This piece represents the apex of his early and rather self-conscious exploration of serial techniques, which had already been used somewhat tentatively in his *Five Pieces for String Quartet* (1949) and more methodically in *Nocturne* (also 1949). A discussion of *Tableau* constitutes a logical conclusion for this chapter, in that the work marks both the end of Freedman's apprenticeship and the beginning of his mature phase as a composer.

The inspiration for *Tableau* was a painting of an Arctic scene that Freedman saw in the lobby of the Winnipeg School of Art. He remembers being profoundly impressed with the mood of the painting, though he can remember neither its title nor the name of the artist. This piece for string orchestra opens with a number of pianissimo unfoldings of a twelve-tone row (P0: 7 9 11 10 1 2 3 8 4 6 5 0) in slow undulating triplets. The first violins enter at Rehearsal A+3 with the opening theme, Freedman's favoured melodic incipit of a rising perfect fourth followed by a rising minor second made possible by his choice of the retrograde form of the row.[13] In example 2-10, note the repeated segments of I5 in the accompaniment, and the overlapped opening and closing pitches of each successive row form.

Example 2-10: *Tableau*, Rehearsal A+2 to A+4

Freedman's row technique in *Tableau* is more sophisticated and varied than in his earlier works. The opening measures exhibit strict, sequential unfoldings of full row forms, each defining an entire measure. Soon thereafter he begins to deviate from a rigid adherence to his series. In addition to reordering the row, Freedman frequently makes simultaneous use of segments from different row forms. There are several important, interrelated motives, each beginning with a perfect fourth. The first motive consists of order numbers 1, 2, 3 or 1, 2, 3, 4 of RPn or RIn, represented in the foregoing example as D G G$^{\#}$ F$^{\#}$ in the first violin. The second motive consists of order numbers 12, 1, 2, 3 of RPn or RIn, seen in the first violin part at Rehearsal F+3 to F+5 as G C F F$^{\#}$. This motive also initiates an expanded form, order numbers 12, 1, 2, 3, 4, 7, 6, 5 of RPn, exemplified in the first violin part at Rehearsal J as F$^{\#}$ B E F E^{b} C$^{\#}$ D G. Note the reversal of the last three order numbers.

Despite a few other such changes in row ordering,[14] Freedman adheres reasonably faithfully to his original version. However, the reader who is consulting the version of the score published in 1960[15] will note several instances in which the composer appears to have inexplicably abandoned any adherence to the row. The explanation is that in making revisions at some time prior to publication he omitted several short segments and altered certain pitches to bridge the result-ant gaps. In the process, he did considerable damage to the integrity of his row, a fact that apparently did not concern him. As we will see in the following chapter, Freedman's enthusiasm for serialism had dimin-ished considerably by the time these revisions were made.

Freedman demonstrates his increasing sophistication in the use of serial techniques by occasionally taking advantage of invariant dyads and trichords to make a smooth transition from one row form to another or to allow different continuations of a single motive. For example, Rehearsal K+5 opens with the motive $G^{\#}\ C^{\#}\ D$ as order num-bers 1 to 3 of RP8, followed at Rehearsal K+7 with the same pitches, now as order numbers 5 to 7 to initiate a statement of RI2.

Tableau contains an early instance of a phenomenon that was to become an important tool in Freedman's writing, the motto chord. From Rehearsal E+1 to E+3 and in numerous other places in the score[16] there appears a chord formed from order numbers 3 to 8 of I1 (example 2-11). At each occurrence the chord is associated initially with a melodic $F^{\#}$ (order number 2 from the same row form). The regular recurrence of identical pitches in exactly the same registers and instruments provides a tonal reference that lends considerable coherence to the work.

Example 2-11: *Tableau*, Rehearsal E+1 to E+3

Example 2-12: *Tableau*, Rehearsal J+1 to K+1

The climax of *Tableau* occurs at Rehearsal K, and Freedman reveals a new skill and intensity in its creation. The section between Rehearsals J and K (example 2-12) is saturated with repeated motivic fragments in two layers, evolving quickly into a complex texture of three discrete and distinct strata. As the texture thickens, the total duration occupied by each motivic repetition in the upper layer is successively compressed from eight eighth notes to four. This, in combination with the thickening texture, displacement of motivic fragments, and gradual increase in dynamic level, creates a powerful and effective climax to *Tableau*, arguably Freedman's finest work up to that point.

Chapter Three
Reaction: The Search for a Personal Language (1953 to 1961)

Nineteen fifty-two had been a watershed year for Freedman. The composition of *Tableau* had marked the culmination of his early and rather self-conscious experiments with serialism as well as his coming of age as a composer in his own right. *Tableau* had been, in a sense, Freedman's ultimate 'homage à Weinzweig.' He soon began to chafe against the restrictions imposed by serialism, and in the decade following the composition of *Tableau* he turned away from it entirely. From his perspective at that time, the mechanics of manipulating the row tended to focus too much of his attention on the notes and not enough on the music. There were many other avenues he wished to explore, and, in his words, 'I had to get a whole lot of stuff out of my system.' It is not surprising that his works during this period exhibit such a remarkable diversity in style. It is worthy of note that even earlier, in the smaller, less pretentious pieces of 1950, 1951, and 1952,[1] he had felt free to eschew serial techniques in favour of a diversity of experiments. In this sense these smaller works align themselves more closely with those discussed in the present chapter.

The years between 1952 and 1960, then, are characterized not only by the rejection of serialism, but also by the quest for a non-serial personal language. The central question to which he sought answers in this period was how to integrate his material while still providing a variety commensurate with the length and scope of the work. Serial techniques had become an encumbrance to him at this point, so he sought other solutions to the problem. In some of his works he achieved coherence through a restriction in length, with a commensurate reduction in the number of different elements or compositional techniques needed to achieve variety. In other, more expansive works he achieved coherence through the generation of a number of variants from a limited number of sources, but in these larger works he made use of more traditional developmental techniques as well. It is clear that he also methodically explored devices and techniques that are characteristic of certain composers to see what relevance they had for him. We can perceive the earmarks of such composers as Bartók, Debussy, Prokofiev, and Stravinsky in many of Freedman's compositions of this decade.

Ironically, following his studies with Weinzweig, Messiaen, and Copland, Freedman had an opportunity in 1953 to expand his understanding of serial techniques with one of its leading proponents, Ernst Krenek, who was teaching that summer at the Toronto Conservatory of Music. Freedman had by this time become more than a little ambivalent about the usefulness of serialism in his own writing. Considering Krenek's own deep commitment to the technique,[2] it is surprising that he made little attempt to influence Freedman to reconsider his opposition to it. Instead, he focused his teaching on the necessity for an appropriate relationship between the material of a composition and the function for which it was intended. Freedman says he learned how important that lesson was when he showed Krenek sketches for various movements of a projected viola concerto. Krenek felt that the material Freedman showed him did not lend itself well to concerto treatment, but would be more suitable for a symphony. Freedman agreed, but did not pursue the idea until the summer of 1960, at which time he found a more appropriate home for some of that material in his *Symphony no. 1.*

In 1954 Freedman was offered a tuition scholarship to study with Darius Milhaud at Aspen, but he had to refuse it because he couldn't afford to pay room, board, and transportation.[3] At this time he was also engrossed in the composition of his *Two Vocalises*, a short work for soprano, clarinet, and piano commissioned by clarinettist Avrahm Galper. There is, of course, no text provided for the soprano, and Freedman does not provide any indication of the kinds of vocal sounds the singer is expected to produce. Freedman had first encountered this kind of textless vocal usage in Duke Ellington's 'Creole Love Call,' 'Transbluesency,' and 'Minne-ha-ha,' but it was his wife, well-known Canadian soprano Mary Morrison,[4] who encouraged him to enhance this technique by using the human voice as an instrument in its own right. In *Two Vocalises*, the first fruit of this new perspective, the voice is indeed treated instrumentally, with the degree of virtuosity of the clarinet and vocal lines virtually identical.

While these pieces are clearly not serial, however liberally the term may be applied, certain aspects commonly associated with twelve-tone serialism can be discerned. The thematic material tends toward encompassing the aggregate within a short space of time, particularly in the first piece. One illustration of this tendency can be found in the piano theme, whose first eleven notes incorporate eleven different pcs. There are two thematic elements in the opening ten measures of the movement, labelled 'a,' and 'b' in example 3-1. Element 'a' appears along with three variants,'a^1,' 'a^2,' and 'a^3.' 'Note the intervallic change in 'a^1' brought about by octave displacement, and the more profound changes seen in 'a^3' engendered by the interpolation of pitches and consequent alteration in the metrical placement of the original tones. As well, 'a^2' is a retrograde of the second to seventh notes of 'a' with some registral and rhythmic changes.

Later in the movement the thematic elements shown in example 3-1 are presented in a different arrangement, now featuring compression, transposition, and recombination, as illustrated in example 3-2. At Rehearsal 1+6, 'b' recurs in the voice at the original pitch level. Concurrently, the piano presents transpositions of 'a' and 'a^1,' first at t=7, then at t=5. Meanwhile, the clarinet recalls material first heard in the piano at measure 7, now slightly altered. This is a subtle and sophisticated little movement, revealing considerable assurance in the handling of materials.

The second of the *Two Vocalises* features two loosely interrelated lines over an insistent rhythmic pattern of 3+3+2 eighth notes in the piano. There is also a veiled allusion to one of the melodic idioms of jazz, shown under the brackets in example 3-3. Freedman is still hesitant to allow his natural proclivity toward jazz to appear in overt form in his compositions.

Fantasia and Dance is Freedman's longest and most ambitious composition to that date. Since he planned only two contrasting movements over a seventeen-minute duration, he faced to a degree unprecedented in his previous experience the dual challenge of integrating his materials while at the same time providing an appropriate degree of diversity. He responded to the first part of the challenge by severely restricting the scope of his source materials, and by subjecting them to only the most subtle transformations. While these transforma-

Example 3-1: *Two Vocalises*, Movement I, measures 1 to 11 (the score is in C).

Example 3-2: *Two Vocalises*, Movement I, Rehearsal 1+5 to Rehearsal 1+10

Example 3-3: *Two Vocalises*, Movement II, Rehearsal 7+3 to 7+8, soprano line

tions in themselves did provide a certain amount of variety, Freedman
turned to another resource to further diversify and enrich the work. He
wrote for the largest orchestra he had ever employed, including several instruments he had never used before, such as alto flute, piccolo,
trombone, vibraphone, deep and bass drums, and suspended cymbals,
with the result that he had a greatly expanded palette of colour to
enhance the variation process. Freedman himself describes this work
as 'impressionistic, with overtones of Hindemith and Stravinsky.' Certainly the manner in which he used the strings (often muted, or in harmonics) and brass (muted, or in glissandi) recalls similar treatments by
Debussy and Ravel, as does his astute use of bass clarinet, alto flute,
and harp to lend a mysterious, almost exotic flavour to the writing.

One of the most interesting aspects of both movements of this work
is the subtle and progressive elaboration of materials. The first movement, *Fantasia*, owes its coherence to a severely restricted collection of
source materials, presented, as is so often the case with Freedman,
right at the outset. Example 3-4 contains the first fourteen measures of
the solo violin part, along with the trombone entry in measure 14.
Omitted from the example are a supporting B pedal in the strings and
timpani, and imitative punctuations of the violin opening in bass clarinet and muted horn.

There are two motivic sources, 'a' and 'b.' Of particular interest is
motive 'b,' whose twisting contour evidently proved so attractive to
Freedman that it became a significant melodic feature of many subsequent works. Motive 'b' in this instance is a representation of pc set class
4-5 (0126). With its subset, pc set class 3-5 (016), it provides the intervallic
basis of much of the material in the opening fourteen measures. When
the trombones join the solo violin at measure 14 the resultant chord
encompasses two representations of pc set class 3-5.[5] Later in the movement Freedman revisits and transforms the trombone chord. Transposed
at t=9, it provides the lowest, middle, and highest tones of a cluster chord
that underscores ten consecutive measures, of which example 3-5 shows
the first. This marks an early occurrence of a cluster chord, a device that
was to become a prominent feature in Freedman's later works.

Example 3-4: *Fantasia and Dance*, Movement I, measures 1 to 14

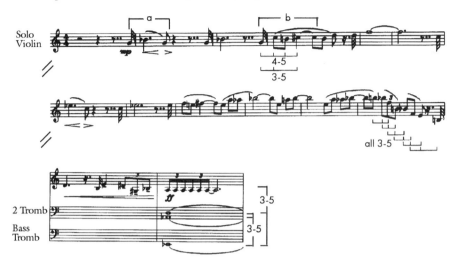

Example 3-5: *Fantasia and Dance*, Movement I, Rehearsal D+3, first and second violins

At about this time Freedman became interested in introducing young people to music. He served as host of the music segment of a television show called 'Junior Roundup,' and also wrote *Laurentian Moods*, a suite of French-Canadian folk songs arranged for high school band. An interest in writing for and working with young people has been strong throughout Freedman's career. He recently expressed his regret that he has not had time to do more in this area.

He also began writing music for films, television, and theatre. In 1956 he provided the incidental music for a television documentary by John Hirsch called *Shadow of the City*, followed in 1957 by the music for a feature film directed by Julian Roffman entitled *The Bloody Brood*.[6] A further foray into the world of film music occurred in 1958, when Freedman supplied the incidental music for a television documentary directed by Doug Leiterman entitled *The Doukhobours*. Creating music for a film requires a special kind of discipline on the part of the composer, who must respond to the demands of the narrative and action by filling a precisely measured time span with music of a specified mood. As well, the composer must be prepared to alter that mood, perhaps dramatically, at a particular moment in time. Freedman's experiences in writing for film are reflected in the way he approaches serious composition as well, as we shall see later when we examine the sketches that he prepares as a means of generating source material and organizing the shape of his works.

Images is the first work written by Freedman following an extensive stint of film writing. Certainly each of the movements has a distinctive and highly dramatic character. Freedman denies any direct influence of the film medium on either the genesis or working out of *Images*, though one suspects at least an unconscious conceptual transfer from one medium to the other. However, it was to the visual arts that Freedman turned for his inspiration in *Images,* just as he had earlier in *Tableau*. Each movement of *Images* is a musical representation of a painting by a Canadian artist. According to Freedman, the first movement depicts *Blue Mountain* by Lawren Harris, the second, *Structure at Dusk* by Kazuo Nakamura, and the third, *Landscape* by Jean-Paul Riopelle.[7] Freedman was aware that Moussorgsky had preceded him in attempting to portray paintings in music, but whereas Moussorgsky's *Pictures at an Exhibition* incorporate literal representations of the artists' work (for example, the sounds of bells in one movement, and of chickens in another), Freedman's *Images* are intended as abstract representations of his models. As the composer states in the Preface to the Berandol edition of *Images*, he is 'not so much concerned with the content of the paintings (two of them are in fact non-objective) as with their design – that is, in line, colour, and mood.' George Proctor is of the opinion that Freedman actually does incorporate a certain amount of literal portrayal of the paintings in *Images*. He comments that for the most part 'the depiction is general rather than specific, although the opening of "Blue Mountain," with its six-bar crescendo from *ppp* to *fff* culminating in a snap-motive (the dramatic cloud over the mountains), would tend to indicate at least some degree of concrete representation of the visual in sound.'[8] However, it is difficult to understand how a 'dramatic cloud over the mountains' is being literally represented by the means Proctor suggests, particularly in the light of Freedman's views about the kinds of physical phenomena that can actually be imitated in music. In an undated paper found among his early sketches, he concludes that music can only be a literal representation of 'things which have a unique *sound*,' or of 'movements which suggest *line* or *atmosphere*.'

Images is one of Harry Freedman's best-loved works. The first movement has proved to be particularly popular, perhaps partly because of a perceived resemblance to the opening of Strauss's *Also Sprach Zarathustra* with which the popular film *2001, A Space Odyssey* begins.[9] Both scores feature in their opening measures two imperious and commanding chordal gestures, each consisting of two dense, dissonant, triple forte chords in a 'scotch snap' rhythm. In the case of the Freedman work (see example 3-6), each chord contains five different pcs, but sixteen distinct pitches, spread over a six-octave span.[10] The pcs C, $C^\#/D^b$, F, $F^\#/G^b$, and G are particularly prominent by virtue of both doubling and placement at the registral extremes. The melodic G^b to F in the piccolo forms the upper boundary of the chord succession, and is doubled in three other octaves by flutes and trumpets. The melodic G to C in the contrabassoon forms the lower boundary, doubled an octave higher by the cellos. The other prominent element is the pc $D^b/C^\#$ which is sustained through both chords in four different octaves (flute, horns, bass clarinet, and trombone).

The significance of these five pcs (C, $C^\#/D^b$, F, $F^\#/G,^b$ and G) becomes clear when the thematic material begins to unfold at Rehearsal 1 (see example 3-7). The theme played by the first violins from Rehearsal 1+1 to Rehearsal 1+3 focuses on the pitches C, F, and $F^\#$. A retrograde of the opening measure at t=1 (G, $F^\#$, and $C^\#$) appears in the second violins immediately thereafter (from Rehearsal 1+4 to Rehearsal 1+5). Later in the movement (Rehearsal 2+1 to 2+8) an elaborated and transposed version emerges in the English horn, which focuses on the pitches D^b, C, and G. Each of these trichords is a representation of pc set class 3-5 (016), and among them they use all five of the prominent chordal pcs C, $C^\#/D^b$, F, $F^\#/G^b$, and G. Three of the five possible such combinations have thus been used thematically in the measures immediately following the opening chordal gestures.[11] The result is a degree of integration between harmonic and linear materials which has not been achieved by Freedman in any of his earlier works.

Example 3-6: *Images*, Movement I, beginning to measure 8

Let us now consider the structure of the theme itself, in its initial presentation from Rehearsal 1+1 to Rehearsal 1+9 (example 3-7).

Subtle motivic and rhythmic relationships are evident among the component segments of this opening theme. Looking first at melodic motives, we recognize immediately the familiar rising perfect fourth followed by rising minor second motive (a version of pc set class 3-5) in the first violin, 'a(P),' followed in the next measure by its exact pitch retrograde, 'a(R).' The third full measure of the first violin part features a modification of measure 2, 'a(R)^1,' while the fourth measure introduces a new motive, 'b(P).' Measures 3 to 4 and 6 to 7 are straddled by 'a(R)' at t=11. The fifth through seventh measures of the first violin part

Example 3-7: *Images*, Movement I, Rehearsal 1+1 to 1+9

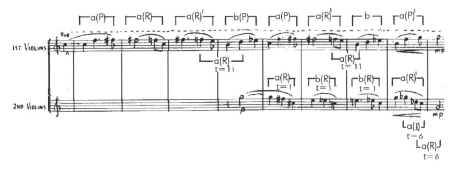

are a compressed rendition of measures 1 to 4 (with measure 2 omitted), and the eighth measure is an intervallically expanded version of the first, 'a(P)¹.' The second violin imitates the opening motive of the first violin in retrograde at t=1, followed in the next measure by motive 'b,' also in retrograde at t=1. As in the first violin part, the final measures of the second violin line are modified versions of its opening measures, and include two embedded statements, 'a(I)' and 'a(R),' at t=6 and t=7, respectively. In order to provide further variety within this restricted intervallic environment Freedman sets his motives in six subtly varied rhythmic patterns. This deceptively simple passage amply demonstrates Freedman's growing skill and subtlety in spinning out a very modest amount of source material into a cohesive unit.

The painting that inspired the second movement of *Images*, Nakamura's *Structure at Dusk*, is described by Lee Hepner as a myriad of 'pale criss-cross lines.'[12] Freedman represents both the colours and the lines of the painting with considerable skill and finesse in this movement. To capture the subtle colours of the painting he omits or mutes the more obtrusive instruments (e.g., trombone, bass trombone, trumpet, piccolo) and deploys all his instrumental resources in a restrained and understated manner. The painting's intricate and delicate linear design is depicted by soft undulating figures, muted trills, and gently inflected chords, interrupted only occasionally by louder passages or sudden silences.

The movement opens with a muted shimmer of sound provided by a trilled pianissimo chord in the upper strings. This opening simultaneity is a form of pc set class 5-20 (01378), with subset pc set class 3-5 highlighted in the first and second violins as the upper pitches of the chord. This subset and five other subsets (pc set classes 3-2, 3-8, 3-9, 4-8, and 4-Z29) are also prominently represented among the various dovetailed undulating figures that emerge in the upper woodwinds above the sustained opening chord in the opening twenty-two measures.

In an interesting passage between Rehearsal 9 and 14[13] Freedman experiments with several new ideas, evidently as a means of portraying the intricate and subtle relationships among the lines in the painting. This is his first attempt at organizing a large segment of a composition around a single process – in this case an extended *bogenform*. Although the techniques he uses to create the arch are not as comprehensive or strict as they would become later in his career, they are nonetheless interesting as a first experiment with logical process on a large scale. Dynamics are the most obvious aspect of the process, the passage being constructed around a large-scale crescendo and diminuendo. The composer presents the performers with a considerable challenge when he instructs them to spread a single 'natural, gradual crescendo and diminuendo' over the entire fifty-one measures of the passage. The first violins, doubled by viola in the first half of the arch and by second violins in the last, provide the leading melodic line, which comprises a series of undulating figures. Each figure consists of from five to nine notes rising and falling to execute a single waveform. Individual figures thus replicate visually and aurally on a small scale the large waveform created by the crescendo and decrescendo that occupies the entire passage. As the climax approaches, successive waveforms in the strings become higher in pitch and their salient pitches are reinforced by the winds. Initially, each melodic waveform consists of either six or nine eighth notes and occupies a full measure, thus reinforcing the pulse. However, as the tension builds the number of notes in each waveform is progressively reduced from the norm of six or nine triplet eighth notes to seven, six, then five, thus seriously destabilizing the established pulse. The resultant conflict between the musical surface and the underlying metre fuels the drive toward the apex of the arch. Example 3-8 shows the five measures leading up to the climax.

Also illustrated in example 3-8 is a further manifestation of Freedman's new interest in process, the pervasive use of heterophony. The 'leading' waveform, built from triplet eighth notes, is shadowed through most of the passage by duplet eighth notes and quarter notes. Heterophony arises because the triplets, duplets, and quarter notes all

Example 3-8: *Images*, Rehearsal 11–1 to 11+4, strings only

traverse the same ground, each slower layer being an eroded version of the material in the next faster layer.

The composition of *Images* was followed in 1959 by a spate of soundtracks for television and film documentaries. However, beginning in the early 1960s Freedman began writing scores for dramas as well, a shift in focus that undoubtedly necessitated a tighter relationship between the music and the action on the screen. It is perhaps significant that during the 1960s Freedman began generating what might be described as a set of program notes as part of his working sketches for his independent compositions. These were essentially narrative chronologies of musical events, as he envisioned them unfolding. We will soon have occasion to examine some of these sketches in detail.

Freedman considers the *Symphony no. 1* (completed on the 23rd of August 1960, published by Berandol in 1961) an important landmark in his career. Just as, in his own mind, *Tableau* marked his 'coming of age' as a composer, he feels that this symphony constitutes a fitting summation of the work of the previous decade. In one sense, he is paying deliberate homage to his illustrious predecessors by adhering to many of the time-honoured symphonic traditions. The work is in the usual four movements, of which three are quite conventional in mood and structure, despite Freedman's assertion that he did not set out deliberately to make use of traditional formal models.[14] In the fourth movement, however, he does break definitively with formal stereotypes in choosing a slow, fugal movement as his finale. In other ways, too, he departs from the Romantic symphonic tradition, as we shall see.

A potentially misleading statement about Freedman's *Symphony no. 1* needs to be qualified here. The authors of the article on Freedman in the most recent edition of the *Encyclopedia of Music in Canada* state that 'Freedman turned away completely from the 12-tone technique in his *Symphony no. 1.'*[15] The reader of this statement would be forgiven for inferring that the symphony in fact marks a departure in this regard. However, as noted above, not one of Freedman's compositions since *Tableau* (1952) has used twelve-tone serialism.

The musical language in this symphony owes much to Bela Bartók, as correctly noted by several writers. In his review of the first performance, *Washington Post* critic Paul Hume comments that '[t]he influence of Bartók is strong in the symphony, both in orchestral sound and in the powerful employment of melodic lines moving in contrary motion.'[16] George Proctor concurs, stating that 'Freedman's *Symphony No. 1 (1960)* also follows the large-scale orchestral tradition. Classical in construction, with much evidence of orchestral colour and rhythmic vitality, the work shows the influence of Bartók.'[17] In fact, Freedman had spent the summer prior to beginning work on the symphony in a detailed study of a number of Bartók's compositions, among them his *Contrasts, Divertimento for Strings,* and *Concerto for Orchestra,* to all of which he freely acknowledges his debt.

In many respects the first movement is the most conventional of the four. The opening theme is an aggressive contrapuntal treatment of two distinct elements (example 3-9). The first consists of a falling minor third or minor second punctuating a series of driving repeated notes in the upper strings. These are reinforced on the downbeats by fortissimo chords, representations of pc set class 3-5 (016). The second element, which soon intrudes in the lower strings, is equally combative, featuring the 'twisting motive' that was first noted in the discussion of *Fantasia and Dance.* Both elements later appear in inverted as well as original form, perhaps a remnant of Freedman's earlier preoccupation with serial techniques.

Rehearsal 7 heralds a complete change of mood, with a new lyrical theme in the cellos sandwiched between upper and lower B^b pedals in the winds and basses. Unlike the opening thematic material, this new theme is periodic in structure, falling neatly into four four-bar phrases. Each begins with a representation of pc set class 3-5 (example 3-10).

The movement as a whole is a virtual catalogue of the classic techniques of imitation, inversion, fragmentation, and recombination. There is an almost studied deference to traditional developmental techniques, almost as though Freedman were attempting to prove to the world that he had indeed mastered the necessary skills to handle

Example 3-9: *Symphony no. 1*, Movement I, measures 1 to 7, strings only

Example 3-10: *Symphony no. 1*, Movement I, Rehearsal 7+6 to 7+21, cello theme only

the symphonic medium. The formal design of this movement also adheres to a traditional model. With its two contrasting thematic ideas, which are recapitulated following a middle section, aspects of sonata form are clearly present, though the middle section is not really any more developmental than the so-called expository sections. The movement is summed up conventionally, with first the original then the inverted form of the twisting note motive, culminating in a final triple forte B^b doubled in multiple octaves.

After the powerful motivic statements that ended the first movement, the second offers a complete contrast. It opens quietly, slowly, and athematically. Freedman's new interest in process is evident right at the outset, when he uses divisi strings to build cumulatively a series of chords in several rising steps. The first occurrence of the process (measures 1 to 7) spans the distance from G^2 to C^4 in two steps. Example 3-11 shows the second, more extensive occurrence, which is higher in pitch and spans a greater distance, from G^3 to F^5.

Example 3-11: *Symphony no. 1*, Movement II, Rehearsal 1+1 to 1+7

In its third occurrence (Rehearsal 2+1 to 2+5) the process is intensified still further. The single cumulative pitches are replaced by cumulative chords, culminating in a twelve-pitch chord with eight different pcs.

From Rehearsal 8 to Rehearsal 10 Freedman sets up a particularly effective process to drive the music toward a climax, expanding upon techniques he had explored in the second movement of *Images*. The excerpt focuses on pcs B and F, with many of the individual gestures emanating from B and incorporating the melodic tritone B-F. Example 3-12 shows the principal players in the drama, the violas and violins, and omits subsidiary material and doubling in the other strings and winds. The climactic chords at Rehearsal 10+1 (not shown) are performed by flutes, horns, trumpets, trombones, and tuba, prepared in the preceding measure by a molto crescendo roll in the bass drum. The first five measures of example 3-12 consist of a semi-imitative dialogue between violas and first violins. Freedman deliberately avoids strict imitation by the reversal of some dyads when they are reproduced in the trailing part, and by the periodic insertion of material in order to alter the temporal relationship between the two parts (as shown in the example). The final measures of the excerpt feature two ostinati which are different from one another, though they share the same incipits (pcs B to F to B) to delineate clearly the onset of each iteration. However, the overall effect is distinctly murky, since the ostinati are out of phase with each other, with the prevailing metre, and also with the articulation. The resultant disorientation and compression, coupled with an increase in dynamic level and doubling, bass drum roll, and chordal support from the winds, provide a powerful impetus toward the homorhythmic fortissimo chords of the climax. In this brief passage Freedman demonstrates his increasing level of sophistication in the craft of building an effective climax.

Example 3-12: *Symphony no. 1*, Movement II, Rehearsal 8 to Rehearsal 10

The third movement is in ternary form (A B A^1). Freedman adheres to the classical ternary model in that the material of the middle section is virtually unrelated to that of the outer sections of the form. The principal materials of the opening A section (labelled 'a,' 'b,' and 'c' in examples 3-13.1, 3-13.2, and 3-13.3, respectively) all feature an identical rhythm of steady eighth notes in 8/8 metre, asymmetrically divided into 3+3+2 eighth notes. Initially the three thematic ideas are distinguished by their intervallic structures, though as the section develops the intervallic distinctions among them begin to blur. In its initial presentation 'a' is characterized by an anacrusis, an arched contour, triadic outlines, a soft dynamic level, and legato articulation. Theme 'b,' perceptibly very different from theme 'a,' lacks an anacrusis, features an inverted arch, more conjunct movement, a forte dynamic level, and detached accented articulation. Theme 'c' is a close relative of theme 'b,' sharing with it the conjunct movement, forte dynamic level, and detached articulation, but distinguished from it by its opening lower neighbour figure and lack of arched contour. The movement opens with several statements of 'a,' punctuated by soft interjections of subsidiary element 'x' in the flute and muted trumpet (example 3-13.4). At Rehearsal 2 there is a dialogue between 'b,' 'b' inverted, and 'c.' Soon after the opening material returns at Rehearsal 4, 'a' is treated imitatively, then in dialogue with 'c' inverted. This dialogue between the strings and winds continues with material that is neither 'a,' 'b,' nor 'c' but rather an amorphous mixture of the three. The size of the alternating blocks in the dialogue is progressively reduced and the dynamic level is increased to propel the music toward the climactic moment of the A section at Rehearsal 9. At this point a string tremolo and percussion support an arresting brass fanfare that inevitably recalls Aaron Copland's *Fanfare for the Common Man*. Example 13-3.5 shows the trumpet opening of this fanfare, omitting the octave doublings by the lower brass instruments. The fortissimo conclusion of the fanfare ushers in the intense and vigorous Section B (Rehearsal 9+5).

Example 3-13: *Symphony no. 1*, Movement III, thematic material

Like most composers of his generation, Freedman was strongly influenced by the work of Igor Stravinsky. He was particularly fascinated by the famous 'Augurs of Spring' section from the *Rite of Spring*, with its powerful reiterated chords and eccentric syncopations.[18] In Section B of the third movement of his *Symphony no. 1* Freedman borrows from Stravinsky the idea of repeated dissonant chords in steady eighth notes, articulated by irregular accents. The famous chord created by Stravinsky for these passages is actually a superposition of two traditional chords – an E^b major-minor seventh and an F^b major triad. Freedman, on the other hand, eschews any clear reference to tertian harmony. Instead he invents two different, though closely related chords, one for the non-accented beats, the other to mark the accented ones. Like Stravinsky, Freedman uses the strings for the chordal pulse and assigns the brass to reinforce the accented beats. Also, like Stravinsky, he adds a melodic counterpoint, though Freedman's is not a repetitive fragment but, instead, an erratic and emotional melodic overlay for three flutes in unison (example 3-14).

Example 3-14: *Symphony no. 1*, Movement III, Rehearsal 9+6 to 9+11

Section A^1 of this third movement (beginning at Rehearsal 13) reworks and recombines the material of the first section. Rhythmic, intervallic, dynamic, and articulative changes are made to the original material. These appear both singly and in various combinations, a virtual textbook illustration of elaborative techniques. The movement draws to an end quietly with a fragment of the flute theme from Section B played by the cello section alone. The final sustained low C serves as a link to the last movement of the symphony.

Unconventionally, for a symphony, the last movement is slow, about eighth note = 72. Equally unconventional for a final movement are the dynamics, which are soft throughout, beginning piano and diminishing to triple piano. The large-scale decrescendo is intensified at the end when the string players are instructed to drop out, one stand at a time, until only a few stringed instruments remain to bring the work to an almost imperceptible conclusion. The movement is a fugue, though J.S. Bach (whom Freedman freely acknowledges as one of his mentors) would not have acknowledged it as such. As mentioned earlier, a more immediate precursor of Freedman who did have a strong influence on many aspects of this symphony was Bela Bartók. Since Freedman had spent the previous summer analysing a number of his works and would certainly have been aware of his *Music for Strings, Percussion and Celeste*, it is odd that he didn't consider the fugal first movement of that work as a model for his own fugal movement. However, it is clear that he did not, since Bartók's strict adherence to his subject, the logical relationship he preserves among successive entries, and the palindromic structure he creates are nowhere to be found in this movement. Instead, Freedman composes a subject that appears in a number of different guises, related only by common opening material and a shared inventory of motives. The succession of entries does not follow a logical intervallic progression, as is the case in Bartók's fugue; in fact Freedman's subject usually appears at its original pitch level. Certainly the movement does not adhere to Bartók's palindromic model, or indeed to any other traditional model. Even the conventional distinction between expository and episodic sections is blurred in Freedman's fugue, since his subject exists in so many versions. The subject is often rhythmically altered as well, either regularly, through proportional augmentation, or irregularly, with resultant displacement of its original accentuation. There are, however, several conventional techniques in evidence, notably the orderly four-voice exposition of the subject at the opening. There is also a three-voice stretto with one voice in augmentation, as shown in example 3-15. Note that the entries are intervallically identical for the first six notes, but deviate from one another thereafter.

Example 3-15: *Symphony no. 1*, Movement IV, Rehearsal 7+1 to 7+4

Freedman's *Symphony no. 1* is a monumental work, one that, in Freedman's words, 'adequately sums up my work of the past ten years but I can't be sure to what extent it indicates my future direction.'[19] It will be the task of the next chapter to determine the direction Freedman takes in the years between 1962 and 1969.

Chapter Four
The Quest for Independence
(1962 to 1969)

With the successful completion of his monumental *Symphony no. 1* in 1960 Freedman had finally achieved the level of confidence he needed to throw off the legacy of the past and to direct his energies in pursuit of his own voice. He no longer had the sense that his mentors were looking over his shoulder, and that he must therefore conform to their musical beliefs. In the previous chapter we saw how he had almost systematically tried out other composers' techniques and styles as he worked to find his own. In the 1960s, though he continued to study the scores of other composers, both past and present, he no longer attempted to emulate their ideas directly. Rather, he used them to trigger and inspire ideas of his own.

Following a history of ambivalence in his attitude toward serialism, Freedman now set out to explore its compatibility with his own developing musical aesthetic. He first moved in the direction of strict usage of the technique. Then, later in the decade, he retreated toward the more moderate and flexible usage that would characterize his mature compositional style. As well, he was finally able to lay to rest his fear of not conforming to the traditional notions of what constituted 'serious music.' He asserted his independence and demonstrated his growing confidence in his own abilities as a composer by incorporating jazz elements into his compositions, first tentatively and almost apologetically, but later boldly and confidently. Toward the end of the decade he embarked on his first tentative experiments with aleatoric procedures and electroacoustic sound. The former would soon become an important ingredient of his craft, though the latter would ultimately prove to have little attraction for him beyond its novelty. He also exhibited a growing ability to capture in music the dramatic and emotional content of text.

In the years up to 1960, Freedman produced an average of only one or two compositions a year, but his interest in composition continued to grow. During the 1960s, his average rose to two or three compositions per year. His need for more time to pursue his interest reached crisis proportions toward the end of the decade, at which time he finally made the difficult decision to resign his symphony post and devote himself full-time to composing.

The first significant work of this period is *Fantasy and Allegro*, a twelve-minute piece for string orchestra completed in 1962. In this work Freedman began tentatively to experiment once again with serial elements. The *Fantasy* opens with a succession of alternating fortissimo chords reminiscent of the paired opening chords in the first movement of *Images*, though with several differences. On a superficial level, the tempo is considerably slower in the *Fantasy*. More significantly, whereas in *Images* there are five pcs in each chord, two of which are present in both chords, in *Fantasy* there are six pcs in each chord, none of which is present in both chords. This segmentation and completion of the aggregate right at the outset is an immediate and perspicuous indication of Freedman's rekindled interest in twelve tone writing. Further, the hexachords represented in the chords are inversionally equivalent representations of pc set class 6-18 (012578). When the musical idea recurs at Rehearsal 3, inversionally equivalent hexachords are also featured, though they are now versions of a different pc set class, 6-31 (013589). The opening chords return, their individual pitch classes now rearranged, to function as a link at a pivotal point in the work, the juncture between the *Fantasy* and the *Allegro* at Rehearsal 8+10. This is the first of many subsequent works in which Freedman features inversionally equivalent hexachordal pairs, but their use is apparently intuitive rather than intentional. The composer asserts that he chose the pitch class content of the paired chords in *Fantasy and Allegro* for two reasons: he wished to encompass the aggregate, and he simply liked the sound that resulted from that particular allocation of tones among the chords.

In one place in the *Fantasy and Allegro* Freedman experimented with a nine-note partially ordered set. From Rehearsal 13 to Rehearsal 18 the thematic material excludes pcs 5, 6, and 7 entirely, and in most of the thematic occurrences the opening four pitch classes (a representation of pc set class 4-16) recur in the same order.

Another notable feature of this movement is Freedman's first use of pointillism. It is unclear to what degree, if any, he was influenced by its use in the hands of Webern. However, Freedman freely acknowledges the influence of the painter Seurat, whose paintings frequently were composed of small points of light. Freedman was inspired to represent the effect in musical tones by dividing the aggregate among nine solo strings, each repeating a specific pitch or dyad at irregular intervals until the end of the passage. Performers enter one at a time, and are instructed to play their assigned fragment using a short, very incisive pizzicato at a pianissimo dynamic level. As the texture grows more dense the number of attack points in each measure grows also, creating an increasingly agitated *sotto voce* muttering. Freedman was obviously captivated by the effect, since he used it twice in the first movement and, exceptionally, recalled it at the end of the last movement as well. In general he avoids integrating the movements of a multi-movement work in this way. His predilection is to have a specific dramatic idea or mood for each movement, a notion that does not invite the recycling of material.[1] He makes an obvious exception to his normal practice in *Fantasy and Allegro*. Example 4-1 shows the opening measures of the first occurrence of this pointillistic material, omitting the supporting chordal pedal point. The order in which the twelve discrete pitches enter is shown in the example.

Example 4-1: *Fantasy and Allegro*, Rehearsal 6+5 to Rehearsal 6+9

Freedman was working on the *Fantasy and Allegro* and the *Trois poèmes de Jacques Prévert* at the same time, completing both works in

September of 1962. Despite this fact, the two works could hardly be more dissimilar. Throughout his career Freedman has always maintained a distinction in compositional procedures and idioms between those works he considers to be 'serious' and those which are lighter in vein. The *Fantasy and Allegro*, manifestly a serious, large-scale work, abounds with dissonance and intricate compositional methods, and serves as a proving ground for experimental procedures. The music of *Trois poèmes*, on the other hand, was created for texts that are either frankly comical, or, at most, bittersweet in mood. These short, self-contained songs are not abrasively dissonant or procedurally complex; they are, in fact, polished, charming, and essentially rather simple in conception and construction.

In these little songs we see for the first time Freedman's genius for capturing the essence of a text in music. He had written for voice previously, but with the *Trois poèmes* he could, for the first time, tailor all aspects of the music to the text without being constrained by previously written musical material.[2] Often the depiction of the text is literal, as in the third song, 'Page d'écriture,' where the bird as it glides down to play with the children is portrayed by a winding chromatic descent in the violin. Occasionally there is a more subtle depiction of the underlying meaning of the text by means of a veiled allusion to an emotion that lurks beneath the surface. For example, in the second song, 'Déjeuner du matin,' the text is sung by a woman who has just quarrelled with her lover, who has apparently been unaffected by the encounter. He goes about his usual routine, studiously ignoring her while she recounts to the listener in painful detail each of his seemingly normal actions. He drinks his coffee, smokes a cigarette, and dresses to go out, while she bemoans the fact that he does not speak to her. Meanwhile this poignant domestic scene is artfully illuminated by the accompaniment, much of which consists of five-note ostinati in steady eighth notes (bracketed in example 4-2). Given the prevailing 6/8 metre, the contradiction between the surface of the music and the underlying pulse subtly highlights the discrepancy between the outwardly normal actions of the man and the distraught emotional state of the woman.[3] The song ends with fifteen slow repetitions of a dissonant chord, a literal portrayal of sobbing and a particularly poignant portrayal of the woman's grief. The excerpt shown in example 4-2 contains the measures immediately following the introduction to this second song.

Example 4-2: *Trois poèmes de Jacques Prévert*, 'Déjeuner du matin,' measures 5 to 12

Freedman has always had an uncanny ability to transform a practical necessity into an artistic advantage. When the Canadian Broadcasting Corporation commissioned him to write *Chaconne* it stipulated its intention to use it at the end of CBC Symphony Orchestra broadcasts to fill out any remaining time. Therefore, they wanted Freedman to write a work that could be easily truncated, or from which segments could be readily excised. The chaconne format fulfilled those criteria admirably, and also stimulated the composer to explore a new vehicle for variation.

If one were to ignore the domain of pitch in this work, one might believe it had been written in the eighteenth century rather than in 1964. Structurally, rhythmically, and texturally Freedman's chaconne closely resembles those of the Baroque era. However, the pitch organization is quite strictly serial. There are thirteen sections in the work, each establishing and maintaining its own distinct character, much in the manner of traditional continuous variations. The work opens with an unaccompanied announcement of the stately eight-measure chaconne theme, which is simply a rhythmicized linear statement of the twelve-tone row. The second and third sections feature a cumulative addition of voices in fugal fashion, each intoning the theme. Subsequent variations consist of two distinct layers, a slow thematic layer and a faster motivic layer. The solemn chaconne theme is present in its original form in the first four and last two sections, but the increasingly migratory use of the row creates new thematic material and motives from non-adjacent row tones for the middle variations. The piece gains rhythmic momentum, textural density, and registral breadth as it proceeds to a climax. Example 4-3 shows the fourth section of *Chaconne*. The theme is in the clarinet line.

Example 4-3: *Chaconne*, Rehearsal 3 to Rehearsal 4 (The score is in C.)

The date for completion of *Chaconne* is given in Freedman's handwriting at the end of the autograph score as January 1964. As we have seen, the work is quite strictly serial, a fact which calls into question the oft-repeated statement that it was not until the composition of *The Tokaido* later in that same year that Freedman returned, after a hiatus of more than a decade, to the use of serial technique.[4] However, it is certainly true that *The Tokaido* represents the apex of serial rigour in his compositional output.

In 1962 Freedman had enrolled in a course at the Japanese Canadian Cultural Centre in sumi brush and ink painting. He recalls how greatly he appreciated the delicacy and expressiveness of this ancient and ritualistic art form as well as its economy of means. Both the techniques and the Japanese elements influenced him profoundly, providing a direct stimulus for the composition of *The Tokaido* in 1964. The self-discipline demanded by a strict use of serial procedures seemed particularly apt for a lean-textured work with an oriental flavour. The article on Freedman in the *Encyclopedia of Music in Canada* elegantly summarizes his rationale in using strict serialism for this work: 'The paradox of free aesthetic expression attained through formalized conventions of craft – a premise in all oriental art – suggested to Freedman that the strictures of serial technique (which at one time had seemed merely onerous) would be helpful in forging a light but strong musical support for the delicate and passionate but ritualistic oriental verse he had chosen to set.'[5]

The Tokaido is a work for mixed choir and woodwind quintet commissioned by the Festival Singers of Toronto. For his text Freedman chose Japanese poetry that had been inspired by a famous nineteenth-century collection of woodblock prints by Ichiryusai Hiroshige. Each print depicts a particular stopping place on the Tokaido road from Kyoto to Tokyo, and the poems that describe the various scenes are set in the classical Japanese forms of *haiku, senryu,* and *tanka.* Freedman selects nineteen of the fifty-three poems, allocating them among four principal musical sections of four poems each, with the remaining three poems divided between an introduction and a postlude. The subject matter within each of the four principal sections is unified – nature, love, philosophy, and wine, respectively – while the framing texts are more general in character. The poems are separated by interludes which frequently extend the mood of the previous poem or foreshadow that of the following one.

The sketches Freedman made in preparation for *The Tokaido* yield fascinating evidence of his method of generating its tone row. They begin not with various iterations of the twelve-tone row, as one might expect, but with a number of shorter motivic fragments. Of the ten motives that Freedman experiments with at the outset, five are representations of pc set class 5-7 (01267), one is a six-note superset of that set class, pc set class 6-Z38 (012378), and the remaining four can be reduced to sets that differ only slightly from pc set class 5-7.[6] Once again Freedman's predilection for motives based on combinations of minor seconds with perfect and augmented fourths is evident. An interesting point to be made here is that while all of the motives that reduce to pc set class 5-7 share the same contour – a five-note ascent – some of them are versions of the inverted form of that set.[7] From this group of preliminary motives Freedman chooses one, motive C to F to F# to B to C#, as the basis for his twelve-tone row. Contrary to what one might have expected, these five tones do not form the incipit of the row. Instead, they are disposed, in order, as the first, third, fourth, eleventh, and twelfth notes. The evolution of motive into row is unequivocal, since the sketches show check marks over the relevant pitches in the row, with the generating motive directly below. The row, which is the source of all the material in the piece, is shown in example 4-4, with the generating motive aligned beneath it.

The row hexachords are inversionally equivalent, a property which we have noted in many of Freedman's rows, but one of which he seems not to have been aware. He may instinctively be attracted to

Example 4-4: Excerpt from the sketches for *The Tokaido*. The row, labelled by Freedman in his sketches 'BS' (or Basic Set), with the generating motive aligned below.

intervallic combinations that yield inversional equivalence in his hexachords, though he rarely chooses to exploit any of the possibilities inherent therein.[8] Such is the case in *The Tokaido*, though in many other respects his treatment of the row is a virtual *tour de force*. In addition to relying on such standard serial techniques as order rotation, migration, and double function of invariant dyads and trichords, he uses more arcane procedures such as those shown in the following example and figure. Surprisingly early in the piece Freedman deviates from a sequential presentation of order numbers. Beginning at Rehearsal 2 the composer deploys the row in migratory fashion among the instruments. At the outset of the passage each row component is presented in turn, but shortly thereafter Freedman selects every second note, then every third, fourth, and fifth in a somewhat irregular, but certainly not random, pattern. The numeric annotations on the score in example 4-5 are order numbers of P0. The score is in C, and the horn part, being tacit at this point, is omitted.

Example 4-5: *The Tokaido*, Rehearsal 2+5 to 3+4

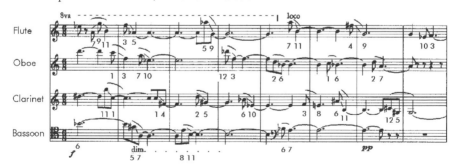

In the following figure, which refers to the portion of the score shown in example 4-5, the numbers in the top line represent the order numbers of P0 as they are deployed in this passage, while those in the lower line indicate the distance in order position between adjacent pitches in the music. Note the grouping 3 3 3 4 which occurs three times consecutively, and the symmetrical grouping 4 4 1 4 4 which follows:

6 7 9 11 1 3 5 7 10 1 4 8 11 2 5 9 12 3 6 10 2 6 7 11 3 8 1 6 11 4 9 2 7 12 5 10 3
 <u>1</u> <u>2 2</u> <u>2 2 2 2 3</u> <u>3 3 4 3</u> <u>3 3 4 3 3 3 4</u> <u>4 4 1 4 4</u> <u>5 5 5 5</u> <u>5 5 5 5</u> <u>5 5</u> <u>5</u>

When I asked Freedman if he recalled exactly how he had arrived at this particular series of numbers he couldn't remember, but conjectured that it resulted from an interaction between two other, more obviously logical series. The reader will remember that Freedman exhibited unusual mathematical ability as a high school student, and has always had a penchant for mathematical puzzles and games.

Another interesting effect was inspired by Freedman's desire to portray simultaneously several layers of textual meaning. In *The Tokaido* his depiction of the text is often undisguisedly literal, a reference to wind being realized musically by glissandi, to rain by pointillistic staccato notes, and so on. But, as we saw earlier in *Trois poèmes de Jacques Prévert*, he is also skilled at a more abstruse representation of the text. His subtle depiction of the following text is a case in point:

> When it's summer / people say
> Winter is the / better season
> Such is human reason.

The irony and perplexity inherent in the first four textual fragments (lines 1 and 2, above) are musically portrayed by setting that text canonically, with cumulative entries culminating in an exasperated unison outburst with the final line of text. The canonic portion (the four fragments of lines 1 and 2) is based on a four-measure, twelve-note theme, using row form I5. Each measure of the theme contains a trichordal segment set to one of the four textual fragments. The voices enter successively at three-measure intervals, repeating the four-measure theme a number of times, so that each measure of this complex texture eventually contains each of the four textual fragments, superimposed. Thus all the requisite textual information is presented to the listener, but in such a manner that it cannot be easily deciphered, a subtle underpinning of the meaning of those lines. The resultant confusion is heightened by the cumulative addition of the instruments immediately following the second vocal entry. Despite an initial impression that the vocal canon is to be reproduced by the instrumental ensemble, the original contour of the theme is soon altered in the leading instrument by registral displacement of many of its constituent pitches, and its identity is further obscured by irregular rhythmic diminution. With the entry of the remaining instruments, the notes of the I5 row are distributed in migratory fashion throughout the texture rather than sequentially in each layer, effectively sabotaging the link between theme and row.

Freedman exploits the harmonic implications of the row to further underpin the irony of the text. When the trichords of the row are superimposed, three conventional seventh chords are formed: in the case of I5 these are $G^{\#}$ diminished seventh, $D^{\#}$ half-diminished seventh, and C major-minor seventh. Each measure of the full vocal texture thus consists of this three-chord succession. However, by the time the full vocal texture is achieved, the instruments have already entered with linearly and vertically compressed statements of the row, thereby undermining the stabilizing effect of the chords (example 4-6).

Example 4-6: *The Tokaido*, Rehearsal 26+5 to 26+8

The dénouement of this intentionally obfuscatory passage occurs when the voices coalesce with unmistakable clarity on the final line of the text, 'Such is human reason,' delivered in bare octaves, *a cappella*. This climactic moment is prepared by two measures in which the text becomes synchronized, and the instruments coordinate with the vocal pitches to allow the three conventional chords which had been omnipresent, though obscured, to be clearly perceived.

While the subject matter and setting of *The Tokaido* lent themselves particularly well to the application of strict serial procedures, Freedman by no means abandoned serialism in subsequent works. The authors of the article on Freedman in the *Encyclopedia of Music in Canada* are correct in stating that '*The Tokaido* became a cornerstone of Freedman's language. Though he wrote no more strict serial works in the next 15 years, he did use elements of serialism – at will, easily and purposefully – in most of his music.'[9]

The *Three Vocalises* of 1964 were commissioned by the Canadian Music Centre for the first John Adaskin Project.[10] In composing the work Freedman had both didactic and musical purposes in mind. In the preface to the score he writes that he wants to 'accustom young performers to new sounds and rhythms,' and by excluding a conventional text he wishes 'to place the emphasis on purely musical elements.' As is usual with pedagogical works and others that he considers to be comparatively lightweight, he eschews complex procedures and textures in favour of more traditional approaches. In fact, in *Three Vocalises* he indulges for the first time in an overt use of jazz idioms. The text consists exclusively of strings of syllables commonly associated with jazz, such as 'ah-bah-lah-doo-wah,' and 'bah-dah-doo-ah,' often given extra impact through syncopation. An equally potent manifestation of jazz influence is found in the third movement in which the purity of the putative key, E^b major, is frequently compromised by flattened third and seventh scale degrees.

In June of the following year Freedman was commissioned by the Festival Singers of Toronto to write *Totem and Taboo*. Unfortunately, it has never been performed,[11] because when their leader, Elmer Iseler, saw the finished product he declared to Freedman that he found it 'too jazzy.' Ironically, the use of jazz is not particularly pervasive in the music itself. The most overt reference to jazz is in the text, where the composer borrowed liberally from the scat sounds of jazz singers. It was apparently to this aspect of the score that Iseler objected.

The sketches for *Totem and Taboo* show the serial use clearly, with row forms and order numbers indicated almost all the way through the forty-four-page score. The row does not have equivalent hexachords, though the initial trichord of each hexachord is a version of the ubiquitous pc set class 3-5. The series is not treated as a theme here, as it is in the *Chaconne*, and Freedman shows himself increasingly willing to compromise the integrity of the row to create a desired motivic shape. For example, to obtain a chromatic descent he inserts two extraneous pitches between order numbers 9 and 10 of RP9 on page 11 of the score. The fascinating aspect of this piece is the manner in which Freedman is able to amalgamate these 'serious' techniques with textual idioms associated with jazz. He uses characteristic strings of syllables such as ah-ba-da-ba and be-dwee-ah-doo within a rhythmic environment characterized by syncopation, changing metres, and polyrhythm.

A Little Symphony (1966) is a particularly interesting work in Freedman's output during the 1960s for several reasons. Not only does he use a single twelve-tone row to govern the domain of pitch in all three conjoined movements, but he uses another kind of series as well. The ten-digit numerical series 3 2 3 2 2 3 3 2 2 3 is applied in a tentative and intermittent manner to the domains of duration and articulation. In this respect Freedman considers his *Little Symphony* to be a preliminary study for his more extensive use of the same series in a work composed the following year, *Tangents*. In *A Little Symphony* the sequence of metres, and the number of measures of each, are frequently governed by the series. For example, beginning at measure 2 there is one measure of 3/4 metre, followed by one of 2/4, one of 3/4, then two measures of 2/4, and so on. On several occasions later in the work the articulation is also controlled by the same series. In example 4-7 the row forms performed by each of the woodwind instruments are articulated in groups of eighth notes defined by the numerical sequence. Note, however, the anomalous groups of three notes in the oboes and second clarinets beginning in the sixth measure of the example.

Scored for large orchestra, *A Little Symphony* calls for an unusually large complement of percussion instruments, many of which are of indefinite pitch.[12] Freedman assigns an important role to the percussion instruments, using them in ways that are entirely new to him. For the first time he allows them to participate equally with the other families of instruments in the presentation of material, rather than restricting them to a supporting role. So important do they become in this work that they are able to hold their own against the other families of instruments in what amounts to a musical battleground in the third

Example 4-7: *A Little Symphony,* Rehearsal 26+4 to 26+13, woodwinds

movement. Beginning at Rehearsal 21+6 battle is joined, with eight highly differentiated blocks of sound succeeding one another in turn. Strings, woodwinds, brass, and various groupings of percussion instruments are starkly juxtaposed, their timbral uniqueness rein-forced by distinctive motives as well. Then at Rehearsal 25+1 common ground is located: several previously heard motives emerge as the vic-tors, to be tossed quickly back and forth between the combatants. The dénouement occurs at Rehearsal 26 when all groups apparently agree to cooperate harmoniously in a quasi-fugal section. From the point of view of instrumentation and orchestration, then, this work is an important landmark in Freedman's evolution as a composer. The size and prominence of the percussion section are unprecedented among his works to this time. Also noteworthy is the new method he evolves here of creating and developing adversarial sound blocks, a method that will become increasingly important in subsequent works.

The years leading up to Canada's centenary in 1967 were extremely productive ones for many of the country's composers. Commissions, plentiful and generous, yielded an abundant harvest of works, many with a distinctly Canadian flavour. One such work was the ballet *Rose Latulippe*, completed in 1966. It was commissioned by the Royal Winnipeg Ballet with the assistance of the Canadian Centennial Commission specifically to celebrate the centennial of Canadian confederation. The scenario was created by Bill Solly and Brian Macdonald, the latter being also responsible for the choreography. Macdonald had previously heard and been fascinated by Freedman's music, and it was he who suggested his name to Sergei Sawchyn, manager of the Royal Winnipeg Ballet, as composer for the ballet.[13] The production schedule imposed a very tight deadline on Freedman, for he was given only two months to write the entire three-act ballet. Despite his initial concern that he would be unable to meet this challenge, he did in fact complete the work in the allotted time. The success of *Rose Latulippe* imbued Freedman with a good deal of confidence in himself as a composer. He remembers being especially gratified to learn that he had acquired sufficient mastery of his craft to work not only well but also quickly. Despite the haste with which the ballet was completed, when he came back to revise it much later he changed very little.

Because *Rose Latulippe* is such an important work in the composer's output, and because many of his compositional decisions and techniques relate directly to events and characters in the story, it will be worth taking a little time at this point to outline the plot of the ballet. The story has all the right ingredients to appeal to the nationalistic pride engendered by Canada's centennial celebrations. Given the location of Expo 67 (in Montreal, Quebec), it was particularly appropriate that the plot be quintessentially French-Canadian, replete with a pious but highly suggestible young girl, her protective mother, her possessive fiancé, and the respected, well-loved, though somewhat farcical family curé. The dark aspect of the tale is furnished by an enigmatic figure known as 'The Stranger,' presumably the devil in disguise. The setting for the ballet is a small village on the north shore of the St Lawrence River in the middle of the eighteenth century. The curtain opens to reveal the home of the Latulippes where the family is assembled for evening prayers with their curé. The Latulippe children, led by Rose, are excited and fidgety because there is to be a dance in celebration of Mardi Gras that evening in the barn. Before he leaves, the curé warns the family solemnly that no one is to continue dancing after midnight, for that is when Lent begins.

Later that evening the sound of sleigh bells heralds the arrival of the guests, slipping and darting across the frozen river. Inside the barn the celebration is soon underway. Dédé, the fiddler, calls a variety of dances, including a reel, a pas-de-deux for Rose and her fiancé Anselme, and a clog dance for eight couples that develops into a contest between the boys. Meanwhile, the older women pass food and whiskey. Rose mischievously tries to take a sip and is reproved by her mother, who is becoming concerned about her daughter's high spirits. Suddenly, sleigh bells are heard again outside. The barn door is dramatically thrown open to reveal an elegant, black-cloaked, Byronic figure. Madame Latulippe politely invites the stranger to dance a minuet with her. Soon he has insinuated himself into the group of young people and begun to flirt with Rose, who finds him irresistible. The jealous Anselme engages the stranger in a contest, which the latter easily wins. Captivated by the handsome stranger, Rose begins to dance with him. Suddenly her crucifix falls to the floor and breaks. The stranger picks it up and offers Rose in its place a jewel from his jabot. As she pins it on her dress she pricks her finger, drawing blood. Anselme, horrified and convinced that the stranger is demonic, rushes from the barn to find the curé. Meanwhile, Rose and the stranger resume their wild and erotic dancing, ignoring the bell tolling the midnight curfew. The curé and Anselme burst into the barn and hurl Rose away from the stranger. Suddenly all eyes turn to Rose, for she has apparently entirely lost her reason. The events of the evening have unhinged her mind, for she no longer recognizes anyone. Seizing the curé's crucifix, she runs out into the snow.

The next scene reveals Rose in an abandoned churchyard, fleeing in terror from imaginary shapes in the snow. In her panic she drops her crucifix, which is found by the stranger. He thrusts it in front of Rose's face, causing her to faint. Stricken with remorse, he wraps her in his cloak, rings the bell in the derelict old steeple to summon help, and then conceals himself. Guided by the sound of the bell, Anselme and the other guests soon find Rose and are able to revive her. Joyfully they discover that she has regained her wits and recognizes them all once again. When she asks how they found her, Anselme demonstrates by pulling the bell rope, but now there is no sound from it. Wonderingly, everyone leaves, convinced that Rose has been saved from the devil by divine intervention. After everyone has gone the stranger comes out of his hiding place, picks up his cloak sadly, and leaves. The ballet ends quietly, with an empty stage and no sound but the wind.[14]

Rose Latulippe provided Freedman with a medium wherein some of the diverse compositional elements and techniques that he had been exploring individually in earlier works could all be accommodated in rich confluence within a single work. We have seen his first tentative explorations with characterization in *Trois poèmes*. In his serious works such as *Chaconne* and *Fantasy and Allegro* we have witnessed his ongoing search for an acceptable solution to what he viewed as the problems inherent in the rigid application of serial ordering. At the other end of the spectrum, we have observed his rejection of any form of serialism in favour of a kind of Stravinskian pandiatonicism in some of his lighter works such as the *Matinée Suite.* In *Rose Latulippe* Freedman found a work sufficiently spacious and diversified that all of these disparate elements could flourish without compromising the integrity of the whole. What we do not see in *Rose Latulippe* is any evidence of the more recent and novel aspects of Freedman's compositional technique: the jazz influences apparent in *Three Vocalises* and the rigidly applied serialism of *The Tokaido.* With respect to the omission of jazz elements, Freedman probably felt that the eighteenth-century setting for the story would have provided a singularly inappropriate environment. The suppression of rigidly controlled serial ordering in *Rose Latulippe* is harder to understand. After all, Freedman had found the technique both appropriate and successful in *The Tokaido.* However, as we shall see, that work would prove to be the last in which Freedman would adhere rigidly to serial ordering. His experience in writing *The Tokaido* evidently demonstrated conclusively to him that this degree of control in the compositional process would become oppressive in the long run.[15]

The score which Freedman composed for *Rose Latulippe* is perhaps less tautly written and certainly more spacious than those of his absolute music. Writing for the ballet, film, or opera manifestly creates a host of different restrictions as well as possibilities for the composer, and Freedman's extensive prior experience in writing film scores proved invaluable to him. The plot of *Rose Latulippe* unfolds briskly with frequent changes in mood, and its principal characters are boldly and colourfully drawn. Given the necessity of mirroring these rapidly moving and strongly contrasted elements with music, it is hardly surprising that Freedman's score is an assemblage of short, well-differentiated sections. Perhaps anticipating a problem with musical coherence, he provided each of his principal characters with a characteristic theme, the periodic recurrence of which provides a bridge between otherwise unrelated musical segments. Further musical linkages are provided by the frequent repetition of segments, either immediately or at some later point in the drama. While occasionally these repetitions are exact, more often they are modified, though rarely extensively enough to obscure their relationship with the original.

The work begins with an overture which, in traditional fashion, tantalizes the audience with snippets from some of the most important musical elements to follow. However, the opening of the ballet is far from traditional in other ways. An essentially chromatic orientation is clear from the very first chord, which contains all twelve pitch classes. The message is clear: despite the setting of the ballet in the mid-eighteenth century, the music will emphatically be a product of the present.

Freedman uses the following twelve-tone row as the basis for most of the work: P0: 0 4 2 3 6 7 8 5 9 11 10 1. The 'strong tonal and folk-like implications' which George Proctor discerns in this row[16] do not appear to me to be particularly striking, despite the fact that ic5 forms the boundary tones of the hexachords. In any case, Freedman rarely highlights that interval class by isolating it musically.[17]

By 1966 Freedman was becoming increasingly convinced that no preconceived compositional process, however elegant, could be permitted to dictate an outcome that was not both appropriate and musically effective. The sketches confirm that much of the pitch material in *Rose Latulippe* is indeed serial in origin, and in many segments of the work the technique is clearly and reasonably strictly applied. In other portions his departures from strict serial ordering are easily traced. Quite frequently one or two pitches are omitted, changed or added to achieve a particular result. A good example can be found at the beginning of Act I, Scene III (page 79 of the score), at which point in the drama the evening celebrations are in full swing. An exuberant mood is created by a background of high trills in the strings around which flutes, clarinets, and oboes weave rapid rising and falling B^b Lydian scales in three displaced layers. The flutes play eight notes per measure, the oboes five, and the clarinets six. Sketches illuminate the manner in which Freedman derived those B^b Lydian scales from his principal series. From row form P8 he initially extracted the following pitches: B♭, D, E♭, E, F, G, A (order numbers 3, 5, 6, 7, 9, 10, 12 respectively), with the missing order numbers appearing in the accompanying string parts. However, in his final version he elected to remove the E♭ and insert a C instead. The missing E♭ does not appear anywhere else, so this action results in an incomplete aggregate. Presumably he effected the change as a purely practical gesture, to secure a stepwise line and facilitate the performance of these rapid scale passages. Elsewhere the ordering is strict.

Another modification that is often encountered is his use of isolated segments of different row forms without placing the missing elements elsewhere in the texture. Despite the frequent appearance of such orphaned fragments, the serial origins of the passages in question are rarely in doubt. A clear example of this can be seen by comparing two similar passages in the ballet. At Rehearsal D (on page 50), when the audience is being introduced to Anselme for the first time, his appearance is heralded by four incisive chords in the strings. His theme is then heard in the first horn (doubled an octave lower by second horn and trombone) with an accompaniment of isolated pitches in the lower strings (example 4-8).

Example 4-8: *Rose Latulippe*, page 50, Rehearsal D+1 to D+8, first horn and strings

The pitches are drawn first from RI8 then from P4, both rows being deployed in migratory fashion between the thematic and accompaniment layers of the texture. However, when Anselme's theme recurs at Rehearsal Q (pages 75–7) the accompaniment is missing, so the theme

is no longer part of a strict unfolding of the row. This is clearly an indication that while Freedman regularly uses a series to generate his
important material he has no qualms about isolating portions of it for
subsequent independent use. On occasion such an isolated fragment is
subjected to further development, effectively obscuring its origins. For
example, when the stranger makes his dramatic first appearance at the
beginning of Act II (Rehearsal B, page 126), Freedman provides several
clear statements of the short theme with which that enigmatic figure is
associated. As in the previous example, the pitches form part of a
migratory deployment of the row, in this case the second hexachord of
I2. Once the audience has absorbed the theme in its original form,
Freedman immediately subjects it to progressive modification, altering
its intervals, its rhythm, and finally even its contour (example 4-9).

Example 4-9: *Rose Latulippe*, pages 126 to 128, Rehearsal B+1 to B+11

In the foregoing instance, the source of the final fragment (which
has little in common with its progenitor) can be determined by the
simple expedient of working backward. However, there are some
places in the score which, though almost certainly serial in origin,
prove far more refractory to analysis. It is possible that Freedman's
manipulations of row ordering were so extensive in these sections that
one cannot determine with absolute certainty which row form was
being manipulated. Another possible explanation is that he was using
an entirely different row or rows for these portions of the score.
Indeed, he admits to having employed supplementary rows in addition to the principal one, and the sketches certainly confirm that he
was experimenting with a number of non-derivative rows at the time
he was planning the work.

As we know, Freedman has always had a fascination with numbers.
During his studies with Messiaen, the young composer was required
to memorize long tables of East Indian rhythmic patterns, an exercise

which he found exceedingly onerous at the time. However, in later years he became aware of the potential of these and other numerical patterns for organizing various aspects of the compositional process. In *Rose Latulippe* there is an interesting example, fully substantiated by the sketches, of the fruit of these early studies. At Rehearsal F on page 164 we are at a point in the drama where it is clear that the stranger and Rose are strongly attracted to one another, but each is dancing with someone else. Freedman, perhaps wishing to hold off for a moment the inevitable contact between that ill-fated pair, underlines the suspense beginning at Rehearsal F+10 with a series of irregularly sized, irregularly spaced melodic fragments in the wind instruments, the initial tone of each fragment being reinforced by a powerfully accented dense chord in the strings and brass. The number of eighth notes in each of the fifteen successive fragments varies, as follows: 9 2 6 3 4 5 3 8 3 5 4 3 6 2 9. This number series is palindromic, but otherwise there is no obvious pattern. However, the series actually emerges from the alternation of two other palindromic series, each of which has its own additional logic. The first series, 9 6 4 3 3 4 6 9, is developed from the decreasing then increasing differences between its successive elements (3, 2, 1, 0, 1, 2, 3 respectively), while the second series, 2 3 5 8 5 3 2, features increasing then decreasing differences between its successive elements (1, 2, 3, 3, 2, 1, respectively). The alternation of these two smaller series produces the fifteen-element palindromic series which Freedman used to produce a convincing sense of suspended animation in this section.[18]

Rose Latulippe provided an occasion for Freedman to explore, however tentatively, two compositional resources that were new to him at that time: electronic sound and aleatoric procedures. Although he had been introduced to electronic music by working briefly in a primitive studio during the 1950s, he had not been inspired to create his own compositions in that medium, or to include electronic sounds within his other compositions. However, when he was planning *Rose Latulippe* he recognized that there were moments in which it would be necessary to create an other-worldly, eerie, ominous atmosphere. He saw immediately how powerfully the atmospheric tension could be enhanced by adding an electronic tape containing icy sounds and a representation of howling wind. The tape he created is not used extensively in the ballet, though its presence at crucial moments adds substantially to the impact of the drama. His foray into the realm of aleatoric music was even more modest, though its importance as a compositional technique was destined to increase dramatically in his subsequent works. However, in this first attempt Freedman limited his explorations to two brief passages, issuing instructions to the glockenspiel player to perform '[a]ny notes in the lower 8ve' (page 43), and later '[a]ny notes in any rhythm; approximately 6 notes to the bar' (page 45).

The innate characteristics of the scenario – the bold strokes with which the principal characters are drawn, the swift pace at which the plot unfolds, and the strong contrasts in mood and setting – created an enticing musical opportunity for a composer of Freedman's abilities and experience. The score that he produced is captivatingly colourful in every dimension – the representation of the mood of the moment, the literal reflection of a given action, the association of each principal character in the drama with an appropriate theme, and, on occasion, even the subtle reinforcement of the plot's hidden message through an apposite compositional procedure. With respect to mood, each unified segment of the ballet has its own distinctive musical character. For example, the scenario calls for a number of dances during the evening's celebrations, and Freedman obliges with a highly diversified group including an energetic reel in 6/8 metre, an elegant 'wrong-note' minuet for Madame Latulippe and the stranger, a romantic and gentle pas-de-deux for Rose and Anselme, and a comical clog dance with a country fiddler style of theme. The clog dance deserves closer inspection, particularly since there is a widespread belief that it is a 'twelve-tone square dance,'[19] a hypothesis that is difficult to substantiate. Like many of the dances in the ballet, the clog dance is based on an authentic Laurentian fiddle tune. Freedman obtained a tape from the National Library containing thirty or forty of these tunes, from which he chose six or seven as models. He copied their exact rhythms and melodic contours, but changed some of the pitches in order to use the total chromatic within a short time span. The pitches in the clog dance, which unfold in a single line for the most part, reveal no recurrent intervallic sequences, making the likelihood of a single underlying series remote indeed. Furthermore, the aggregate is never completed before the reintroduction of tones already heard. It seems doubtful that the clog dance is serial in origin, however liberally the term may be interpreted. Set for solo fiddle accompanied by bass drum, spoons, and an occasional off-beat 'drone' on G or D string, it attains a high degree of internal cohesion through repetition on three levels: motive, phrase, and section (example 4-10).

Example 4-10: *Rose Latulippe*, clog dance, page 97, beginning to Rehearsal A, violin only

There are numerous instances in which the actions on stage are reflected literally in the music. A good illustration can be seen on pages 71-2. As the curé totters across the slippery ice en route to the celebration, trying to keep his balance with little help from the wind, the music echoes his clumsy actions with glissandi in string harmonics along with trills and erratic scale figures in the woodwinds.

In addition to effectively depicting mood and specific actions, Freedman also proves himself adept at capturing the individual personality of each of the principal protagonists in the drama. The themes associated with the various characters are introduced when they make their initial appearance on stage, and are invoked at critical points throughout the drama. Their frequent recurrence serves to bind the work into a musical as well as theatrical whole. The curé's solemn, somewhat pedantic character is represented by repeated chords in half notes. At crucial stages in the narrative these chords sound a warning and serve to alert the audience to impending catastrophe (example 4-11).

Example 4-11: *Rose Latulippe*, page 31, Rehearsal B+1 to B+4

Rose's theme, on the other hand, is a gentle and dreamy waltz designed to highlight her romantic, other-worldly character (example 4-12).

Example 4-12: *Rose Latulippe*, pages 35 to 36, Rehearsal A–9 to A+7

The rough and virile nature of Rose's boyfriend, Anselme, is depicted by four incisive introductory string chords followed by an aggressive theme in changing metres in the horns and trombone, shown earlier in example 4-8. Freedman's early sketches for the stranger's theme reveal that he initially envisioned one that outlined a tritone, the interval historically associated with the devil. He ultimately rejected this theme, perhaps considering it to be too obvious in its reference to the forces of darkness. The stranger was, after all, not irredeemably evil; at the end of the ballet he showed remorse and compassion after witnessing the results of his mischievous interference with Rose. The theme which Freedman ultimately developed for the stranger also outlines a triad, though an augmented rather than a diminished one (refer to example 4-9). It is frequently accompanied by the tones missing from the row in another voice, though just as frequently the principal motive becomes detached from its surroundings and undergoes successive intervallic and rhythmic changes.

In Freedman's hands these themes are normally employed in a relatively uncomplicated manner, serving merely to draw attention to the appearance or action of a particular person on the stage. Although he often transforms the themes to reflect different emotions or situations, the modifications are rarely extensive, being largely confined to alterations in timbre, register, or accompaniment. An exceptional degree of transformation does occur at the point in the drama when Rose and Anselme are dancing a pas-de-deux together (page 99, Rehearsal G). Rose is represented by a solo violin, Anselme by a solo clarinet. In this lean texture, it is easy to hear that elements of both of their themes merge. The changing metres which characterize Anselme's theme and the iambic rhythm of Rose's theme combine in quasi-imitative dialogue, perhaps symbolizing their commitment to one another at this point in the narrative.

There are numerous instances in which Freedman's employment of specific compositional procedures at certain points in the drama invites the analyst to conjecture that they may have been invoked in subtle reinforcement of a deeper level of meaning in the story. In some cases Freedman's intentions seem obvious, for example in the deft manner in which he underlines the hidden message of the plot during the contest between the stranger and Anselme (pages 159–94). The two characters alternate at centre stage as they vie for superiority, and Freedman cleverly symbolizes the progressive defeat of Anselme by causing his segments to grow increasingly abbreviated while those of the stranger gradually expand in length. Another example can be seen in the minuet between the stranger and Madame Latulippe (pages 141–2). The essential 'wrongness' of the stranger's presence and the artificiality of his welcome by Madame Latulippe are graphically portrayed by the 'wrong-note' character of this otherwise deliberately archaic minuet. At other times the connection between the drama and a specific compositional procedure must remain purely conjectural. One such instance occurs in the opening three sections of the Finale. Musically, these cohere as a self-contained unit consisting of an initial section of sixteen bars (page 277–9, to Rehearsal A), a middle section with different material, and a final section in which the initial part is reprised in retrograde (Rehearsal C to D). It is unlikely that an audience would perceive that a retrograde of earlier material was taking place in the third section, particularly since the orchestration is extensively reworked and a twenty-two-measure middle section intervenes. However, Freedman may have been attempting to symbolize subliminally an important underlying message of the scenario. At this point in the story Rose is discovered lying in the snow by Anselme, the curé, and the other guests. Through their efforts they are able to revive her, and are overjoyed to discover that she has regained not only her consciousness but also her wits. Perhaps Freedman's palindrome is a musical representation of Rose's falling from grace and losing her mind, then miraculously being restored again both to her sanity and her faith.

Rose Latulippe is a monumental work that marks a milestone in Freedman's evolution as a composer. The work was aptly described by George Proctor as 'the most significant ballet connected with the centennial celebrations.'[20]

In none of his works up to this point has Freedman relinquished the use of time signatures. Although he has used changing and irregular metres frequently, his *Anerca* of 1966 marks the first occasion in which he risked eliminating metre entirely. Large segments of this work lack not only a metre but also a regular underlying pulse, resulting in a rhythmic freedom unprecedented in his previous compositions. The success of this venture may have encouraged Freedman to embark on further experiments with rhythm in the following year, in *Tangents.*

Tangents (1967) is a set of continuous symphonic variations in one uninterrupted, lengthy movement, subdivided into three large sections on the basis of tempo and mood. The work was commissioned by the National Youth Orchestra Association with the collaboration of the Canadian Music Centre under a grant from the Canadian Centennial Commission. Freedman did not let the youth of his performers deter him from making stringent demands upon their capabilities, both technical and musical. He also describes the work as a veritable 'Cook's tour' of contemporary techniques. As he says in his introductory notes in the score, the players are 'just about ready to become professionals,' and, being young, are 'more receptive to new styles.' Given the latter statement, it is odd that Freedman would not have given more prominence to the use of jazz and aleatoric procedures than he did. There is a brief reference to a popular idiom at Rehearsal 35 where D major and G major 'oompah' chords supporting diatonic fragments from a cheeky childhood taunt temporarily replace the use of the twelve-tone series, but the passage has a closer affinity to rock and roll than to jazz.[21]

With respect to chance elements, there is one measure in the second movement (Rehearsal 14–2) in which the conductor is directed to stop beating time, allowing and even encouraging a lack of coordination between the six soloists. However, since the notes and rhythm are fully written out, the degree of indeterminacy is modest indeed. In two other brief sections in that movement the metre is suspended, though there is no room for improvisation here either, since a regular pulse is maintained throughout, and the performers are allowed no latitude in performing the notes written in the score.

Notwithstanding the virtual absence of jazz and aleatoric elements, the work is indeed a 'Cook's tour' of contemporary techniques. So many are there that one almost suspects Freedman of deliberate pedagogical intent. Certainly young composers and performers of the day would have had much to discover from a careful examination of *Tangents*, from the innovative use of its orchestral colour to the intricate procedures for generating and organizing its materials. In this work, Freedman does not restrict his use of series to the domain of pitch. In fact, he employs two series: the first, a twelve-tone pitch class series (P0: 9 0 8 2 4 3 10 5 11 1 6 7), governs the sequence of tones, while the second, the ten-digit numerical series (3 2 3 2 2 3 3 2 2 3), used earlier in *A Little Symphony*, controls many other aspects of the work.[22]

Although in his introductory notes to *Tangents* Freedman asserts that the work is 'not based on a recognizable theme,' in his sketches he does indeed refer to a 'theme.' In fact, the opening few pages of the score almost inevitably bring to mind the composer's earlier *Chaconne*, a work in which row and theme are clearly associated. Both works begin with successive, slow-paced linear statements of the twelve-note row, each statement featuring different instrumentation. In *Tangents*, however, variation of the 'theme' is already evident in the second statement, which features slight changes in the rhythm and registral placement of some of the notes, and by the beginning of the fourth statement the variation process has begun in earnest. Although the 'theme' remains intact here, each of four textural layers unfolds it at a different level of rhythmic diminution, in the ratio 3 : 4 : 6 : 8 notes per measure, creating a dense, complex texture. Thereafter, despite a quite strict use of serial ordering, the 'theme' disappears, and the row functions exclusively as a source of motivic and accompanimental material throughout the remainder of the work.

The numeric series generates many non-pitch aspects of *Tangents*, particularly in the domains of duration and articulation, though there are instances in which the series controls texture, instrumentation, and metre as well. Several examples should suffice to indicate the scope of Freedman's methods. In example 4-13.1 it can be readily seen that the distance (measured in quarter-note values) between successive pizzicato A^4s in the cello is governed by the series. The distance between successive G^4s in the viola and cello parts (example 4-13.2) is similarly organized, though the unit of measurement this time is the eighth note, and elements of the series are frequently combined to form larger units: 5 (=3+2) 7 (=3+2+2) 3 3 4 (=2+2) 3, etc. Example 4-13.3 illustrates the application of the series to articulation.

Example 4-13.1: *Tangents*, Rehearsal 1+1 to 1+4, cello

Example 4-13.2: *Tangents*, Rehearsal 2+1 to 2+4, viola only

Example 4-13.3: *Tangents*, Rehearsal 36+5 to 36+8, timpani

There is another interesting variation (Rehearsal 26 to 29) in which both metre and articulation are organized by the numeric series. There are six repetitions of the succession of metres 5/8, 7/8 , 6/8, 7/8. Each measure contains steady eighth notes, but the articulation makes it clear that the internal divisions express the numeric series, as follows: 5/8 (3+2) 7/8 (3+2+2) 6/8 (3+3) 7/8 (2+2+3).

In one of the variations close to the end of the piece (Rehearsal 33ff), Freedman uses the numeric series to control texture as well. Against a background of driving eighth notes in the percussion section he alternates massive 'skyscraper' chords consisting of many different pitches with leaner chords containing a single pitch class doubled at the unison or octave. The distances between the alternating chords are determined by the numeric series, measured in quarter notes. A chord with multiple pitch classes that occupies a duration of eight quarter notes (3+2+3 of the series) is followed by a chord with a single pc (seven quarter notes, 2+2+3), then one with multiple pcs (five quarter notes, 3+2), one consisting of a single pc, (eight quarter notes, 2+3+3), and so on.

Tangents, along with the ballet *Five over Thirteen*, composed two years later, represents the outermost limit in Freedman's invocation of mechanical procedures to govern the compositional process, Thereafter, he finds technical restrictions of this kind, even if self-imposed, increasingly counter-productive.

In *Toccata* of 1968, Freedman seems to have cast off the last of his inhibitions about the use of jazz. The adjective that comes to mind in describing *Toccata* is 'relaxed' – relaxed in both technique and idiom. It is a work of modest proportions, both in size and instrumentation. He was writing for two performers he knew very well, flutist Robert Aitken and soprano Mary Morrison, his wife. Since both were experienced with contemporary techniques, he could be confident that his intended performers would adapt easily to his quasi-improvisatory score. The flute and voice interact as equal partners, often sharing the same material. The use of repeated notes is a prominent feature, realized by flutter tonguing in the flute and 'da ba' syllables in the voice. Although a tone row generates the pitch material, it is not applied with strictness, and is even temporarily suspended in favour of unrelated scale flourishes. Frequent metre changes contribute to the unstructured feeling of the work.

Five over Thirteen (1969) is the second of seven ballets in which Freedman collaborated with choreographer Brian Macdonald.[23] The ballet recounts the relationships among five people who physically and emotionally dominate thirteen other people, hence its title. The work is noteworthy in Freedman's output for several reasons: along with *Tangents*, it represents the apex of his preoccupation with mechanical procedures for composition, it marks his first extensive foray into the realm of electronic music, and it provides interesting evidence of his growing confidence in improvisation as a viable compositional tool.

The title of the work suggested to Freedman the possibility of using mathematical models derived from the Fibonacci series to generate or manipulate his material.[24] In typical fashion, he embarked upon extensive research into the nature, origin, and potential application of this series. Photocopies of various articles on the subject are enclosed with his sketches for *Five over Thirteen* along with page after page of pencilled jottings in which he attempts to adapt the series to serve his purposes in a variety of musical domains. In the end his attempts were futile, as he was unable find any application of the series that satisfied him musically. Nevertheless, his preoccupation with the manipulation of integers did lead to the control of various compositional parameters in this ballet by other, less obscure mathematical means, as we shall see.

The work begins traditionally enough with straightforward statements of the tone row, but after a few pages it becomes clear that the sequential presentation of individual row forms has been suspended in favour of the non-sequential presentation of isolated motivic fragments from the row. Moreover, although each short fragment comprises an ordered row segment, there is no single row form that can accommodate all the motives that are being presented at any given time. Nor is it a simple matter of two or more different row forms being heard simultaneously; each motivic fragment is an isolated excerpt from a different row form. The sketches for this work are very revealing, and offer a clue to the manner in which Freedman has adapted serial technique to his own needs. The reader will recall that during the years between 1948 and 1952 the composer used the tone row primarily as a source of motives that could be extracted from their context to function entirely independently. Following a period of rejection of serialism, he turned in 1962 toward a strict use of serial ordering. Now, in the ballet *Five over Thirteen*, we find a return to the motivic approach, the genesis of which is made explicit in the sketches.

The opening staves in the sketches show Freedman's two attempts to evolve a tone row from a set of motives. In his first version he writes out a sequence of twelve motives, the first three of which comprise the opening ten pitch classes of the tone row he ultimately chose for the work. In his final version he substitutes new motives for the earlier fourth, fifth, sixth, and seventh motives, while retaining the other eight. An interesting aspect of this manoeuvre is that he also transposes five of those eight motives from their original pitch levels, thereby annihilating the original row ordering. Specifically, the ten pitches of the first three motives no longer coincide with the first ten pitch classes of his tone row. While each of the twelve motives is an ordered segment of at least one row form, eight different row forms would be required to accommodate them all (Pn, Pn+5, Pn+7, Pn+11, RPn+1, RPn+5, RPn+11, In+5). Freedman wrote some figures above the staves in his sketches which indicate the number of occurrences of each pitch class within the complex of twelve motives. He was evidently concerned to achieve a satisfactory balance among pitch classes and to ensure that none emerged as dominant.

These sketches provide a tantalizing glimpse at the way in which Freedman formalizes an approach that had been largely intuitive prior to this time. A sequence of motives generates the tone row which governs large segments of the work, but subsequent transposition of some of the motives allows them to float freely thereafter, unrestricted by membership in a larger row context.[25]

Example 4-14.1 shows the tone row, example 4-14.2 the twelve motives of the first version, and example 4-14.3 the twelve motives of the second version together with their relationship to the first version.[26] Note that in the second version motives 4 and 5 are shown as a single entity, presumably because the new motive appears at some points as a single line, and at others in the form shown.

The sketches reveal further manifestations of Freedman's use of numbers as a compositional aid in this work. There are numerous charts tallying the number of occurrences of a given element, be it pitch classes, motives, or instruments, within a given time span. The intent seems to have been to avoid the hegemony of any member in a group of like elements. There is a particularly interesting chart in the sketches showing twelve columns of figures in five rows. Each row contains all of the integers from 1 to 12 in a different order, with a tally

Example 4-14.1: *Five over Thirteen*, row from the sketches
Example 4-14.2: *Five over Thirteen*, motives from the first version, as shown in sketches
Example 4-14.3: *Five over Thirteen*, motives from the second version, as shown in sketches

Example 4-14.1

Example 4-14.2

Example 4-14.3

at the side to confirm that each integer has been used once and only once in each row. The significance of this chart is found in the passage from Rehearsal 5+4 to 13+7, where it becomes clear that the figures in the left-hand column refer to instrumental layers in the texture, while the remaining figures refer to the order in which the twelve motives of example 4-14.3 are to be deployed in the associated layer. The five discrete instrumental strata, shown in the order listed by Freedman, are clarinet (layer 1), piano and cello (layer 5), flute and English horn (layer 3), violins and viola (layer 4), and double bass (layer 2). The sketch chart is reproduced below.

1)	9	2	1	10	8	3	4.5	7	6	11	12
5)	4.5	1	11	6	3	12	9	7	8	10	2
3)	4.5	11	3	12	1	10	8	9	6	7	2
4)	8	7	3	4.5	12	2	11	6	10	1	9
2)	2	4.5	8	3	12	9	1	11	6	10	7

Each instrumental stratum performs the twelve motives in a different order, as prescribed in the chart. At the beginning of the passage (page 6) the texture is lean, and each motive is set apart from its neighbours by rests or long durations, thus allowing the individual motives to be easily perceived. Gradually, the motives become less perceptible as more layers are added to the texture. Aural recognition of individual motives is further obstructed as a result of rhythmic changes to each motive and blurring of the boundaries between them. Eventually, the identification of individual motives becomes virtually impossible. The effect at the end of this passage is reminiscent of that achieved by Freedman in a number of earlier works using much simpler means – the cumulative addition of superposed and displaced statements of a single ostinato. Example 4-15 shows the first three entries of the passage, omitting the percussion instrument, which accompanies the motives in a nervous, intermittent tattoo. Note that Freedman deviates from the order of motives prescribed in his chart by reversing motives 3 and 8 in the clarinet line. He also repeats several segments.

Example 4-15: *Five over Thirteen*, Rehearsal 5+4 to Rehearsal 8

In the summer of 1966 the Graduate Department of the University of Toronto's Faculty of Music offered a course in electronic music. Freedman was quick to seize the opportunity to work in the newly created electronic music studio under the tutelage of such prestigious academics as Hugh Le Caine and Gustav Ciamaga. Despite the extremely primitive state of the studio – he recalls one piece of equipment bursting into flame – he emerged from the course filled with enthusiasm for the new medium, and eager to apply his new skills to his own composition. *Five over Thirteen* offered an appropriate venue for his experiments, so Freedman enlisted the technical assistance of Lowell Cross, who prepared a tape for him according to his specifications.

The prepared tape is an important and integral part of the score, accompanying and sometimes interacting with the orchestra. Not only are electronic sounds heard, but there are traditional sounds as well, such as a rock and roll segment with the regular bass filtered out and replaced by electronic sound. The conductor is instructed to become familiar with the contents of the tape, since he must often coordinate the orchestra with it. This is particularly important in a section in which both tape and orchestra execute a series of crescendo/decrescendo segments; the conductor must coordinate the two so that a decrease in volume in the tape is counterbalanced by a corresponding increase in volume in the orchestra. On another occasion, the conductor is explicitly instructed not to coordinate the orchestra with the tape, but to maintain the prescribed orchestral tempo in deliberate opposition to that of the tape. With taped segments present for nearly half of the twenty-minute ballet, *Five over Thirteen* is certainly Freedman's most ambitious and extensive use of the electronic medium to this time. The heightened sensitivity to unusual timbres that resulted from his immersion in the world of electronic sound may have spilled over into his use of conventional instruments as well. For example, at one point the pianist is instructed to strike the strings with mallets, and on another occasion to pound the keyboard with both forearms to form a solid cluster chord.

The use of improvisation is also more venturesome than has been the case in earlier works, with more control being delegated to the performer. The most interesting moment in this respect occurs at a climactic point in the score (Rehearsal 39) during which each player is instructed to improvise rhythmically on a given set of unordered pitches. This is the first time Freedman has allowed his players to choose the order as well as the rhythm in which the given pitches are to be played.

Five over Thirteen seems a logical place to conclude this chapter. The work marks the culmination of Freedman's preoccupation with mathematical means to govern various aspects of the compositional process. At the same time, it is the locus of his first widespread forays into the worlds of electronic and aleatoric music. We have seen that the years from 1962 to 1969 were witness to a number of 'firsts' for Freedman: the first use of pointillism (in *Fantasy and Allegro*), the first overt use of jazz idioms (in 'Chant' from *Three Vocalises*), the first amalgamation of serial and jazz techniques (in *Totem and Taboo*), the first extended suspension of metre (in *Anerca*),[27] the first use of the electronic medium (in *Rose Latulippe*), and the first use of improvisatory writing (also in *Rose Latulippe*). Virtually all of these can be viewed as but tentative beginnings in the more intensive and focused pursuit of these new directions in the following decade.

Chapter Five
New Directions (1970 to 1976)

Following his tentative explorations into the realms of electronic sound, aleatoric procedures, and jazz in the 1960s, Freedman now embarked enthusiastically on a full-scale search for new and exciting possibilities. His determination was undoubtedly fuelled by his new-found freedom to devote himself to composition. In 1970 Freedman resigned his post as English horn player with the Toronto Symphony. He concedes that the orchestra was not unhappy to lose him as a player. He had recently bought an expensive new instrument and was having great difficulty in playing it in tune and getting it to speak properly in certain registers.[1] Providentially, the orchestra was celebrating its fiftieth anniversary in the 1970–71 season, and took the opportunity to appoint Freedman as its first composer-in-residence as a way of commemorating that event. The title allowed both sides to save face, and the salary associated with the position afforded Freedman some form of compensation for the meagre pension that the orchestra paid at that time.

Freedman's growing interest in improvisation found a natural outlet in a commission by the Canadian Broadcasting Corporation in 1970 for *Scenario*. The composer clearly signalled his intention to include jazz elements in the work by his instrumentation, which includes alto saxophone, jazz set, electric bass guitar, vibraphone, and a battery of percussion instruments in addition to a full orchestra. The work is an eclectic mixture of serial and jazz techniques. Like his other contemporaneous works, this one exhibits a rather casual approach to serial ordering and a tendency to extract motivic segments from the row for independent use. The strong jazz orientation results not only from the use of the jazz instruments themselves but also from the incorporation of typical jazz idioms such as walking pizzicato bass lines and highly syncopated melodies set against strong repetitive downbeats. The essentially jazz orientation of *Scenario* was particularly conducive to improvisation, which Freedman used to a degree unprecedented in his output to this time. He would have been confident that players of jazz instruments, in particular, would have the ability to improvise effectively, but he clearly was less certain about the abilities of traditional orchestral players in this respect, since he imposed greater restrictions on this group. Example 5-1 provides representative aleatoric excerpts from the score. In example 5-1.1 the second violins, as part of a larger group of similarly deployed stringed instruments, are divided and assigned a set of pitches on which to improvise for a specific period of time. In example 5-1.2 the string players are accorded a similarly modest degree of choice. Here each player is directed to choose any pitch within the circumscribed range, the result being a dense cluster chord. In contrast, example 5-1.3 gives a clear idea of the greater amount of freedom given to certain players, particularly those who would likely have had considerable experience in the jazz field. The improvising percussion players[2] are instructed to 'listen to one another in order to achieve a group improvisation rather than 4 separate, independent parts.' On other occasions the alto saxophone is asked to improvise on a chord, such as the D^{7b10} chord at Rehearsal 11+3, or simply to improvise, with no directions or restrictions, as at Rehearsal 31.

Example 5-1.1: *Scenario*, Rehearsal 1+5 to 1+8, second violins divisi

Although *Scenario* is a showpiece of aleatoric writing, the work as a whole seems to overflow with disparate materials and techniques, not all of which cohere successfully. For example, beginning at Rehearsal 13 a languid solo in the alto saxophone is followed by a series of measured chords in the harp. A walking pizzicato bass joins the harp chords along with an improvisation by the alto sax. Meanwhile, various instruments enter cumulatively to form a number of different cluster chords, followed by a statement of the opening thematic material in

Example 5-1.2: *Scenario*, Rehearsal 31+11 to 31+18, strings

Example 5-1.3: *Scenario*, Rehearsal 16+2 to 16+11, bass guitar (bottom stave) and percussion

the bass guitar, all within a short time frame. One senses that Freedman found it difficult in this work to curb the number and scope of the ideas he wanted to try out.

The success of the aleatoric sections of *Scenario* undoubtedly paved the way for a more extensive employment of improvisation in an otherwise more conservative work, *Klee Wyck*. Completed in November 1970, *Klee Wyck* was inspired by the paintings of Emily Carr. The title translates as 'The Laughing One,' which is the name bestowed upon Carr by one of the Indian nations at which she was a frequent visitor. Freedman acknowledges his own long-standing admiration for Canada's native peoples by incorporating several authentic Indian melodies into *Klee Wyck*.[3]

One of the most striking aspects of this composition is its extensive and ambitious use of aleatoric procedures. Since his early cautious experiments in *Rose Latulippe*, Freedman had been using these procedures with steadily increasing confidence. He had relied heavily upon the improvisational skills of jazz musicians in *Scenario*, but with *Klee Wyck* aleatoric procedures take their place in traditional symphonic music as a vital and integral component of his craft. In no fewer than twenty of the thirty-five pages of this score, the players exercise some degree of control over the outcome through improvisation of various kinds. In the opening few pages the strings are divided into eleven parts, each instructed to improvise on its own group of notes. The parts enter cumulatively until, at the climax of the passage, all the string players are improvising simultaneously. The composer's instructions for the passage are as follows: 'All improvisations should be as fast as possible and in irregular rhythm. No attempt should be made to co-ordinate the several players playing each line. ... The improvisations must retain the order of the given notes.' Since a number of players are assigned to each of the eleven parts, and each performer improvises independently, the result is a dense and undifferentiated sound mass. Freedman evidently found this technique very effective, since he made use of it often in subsequent works. In another aleatoric passage (from pages 12 to 16) stringed and woodwind instruments participate individually in a series of overlapped flourishes of ten to fourteen notes apiece. Cued by the conductor, regular pulse having been suspended, the players perform their assigned notes at approximately the tempo indicated, but they are given their own choice with respect to articulation and rhythm. The tempo of successive flourishes increases incrementally, from quarter note = 72 to double that speed at the end of the passage.

Improvised cluster chords of the kind used in *Scenario* (illustrated in example 5-1.2 above) are given a far more prominent role in *Klee Wyck*. A lengthy section of the work (from Rehearsal 11 to Rehearsal 18) features adaptations of authentic Indian melodies. In addition to those that are written as single lines and hence easily perceived, there is another melody, heard throughout the passage, that functions as a thickened counterpoint. In example 5-2, the lower strings execute a vigorous and strongly accented tune, the precise pitches of which are effectively obscured. Freedman accomplishes this by directing each player to choose any starting point within the given range for the performance of the melody. As a result only a generalized contour is discernible. Freedman had used these cluster chords in *Five over Thirteen* and in *Scenario*, but their purpose had been primarily harmonic rather than melodic. Example 5-2 shows the opening five measures of this lengthy passage in *Klee Wyck*. While the violins perform one clear and unequivocal Indian melody, the lower strings collectively perform another that can be perceived only as moving and rhythmicized shape.

Example 5-2: *Klee Wyck*, Rehearsal 11+1 to 11+5

There has been little discussion thus far of the many works that Freedman has written explicitly to appeal to young students. The composer has always had a strong interest in opening the hearts and minds of youth to contemporary musical sounds. Works such as *March?*, *Scales in Polytonality*, and *Four Pieces for School Band* are noteworthy both for their innovative musical sounds and techniques and for their accessibility to young audiences and performers. Freedman frequently achieved these goals by introducing a limited number of novel elements within an otherwise traditional context. In *Keewaydin* of 1971, however, he abandons this concession to conservative taste and plunges his young people headlong into a new sound world. The work was written for the Bishop Strachan School Choir of Toronto, a group that must have been both highly skilled and unusually adventurous. The Preface to the published edition of the work[4] includes the following description: 'The purpose of the piece is to prepare young people for contemporary musical experiences by stressing intervals and interval relationships rather than notes of a scale. It is, in this respect, an ear training piece, requiring as it does the development of a fair degree of pitch memory as well as the ability to sing any interval – particularly major and minor 2nds and 3rds – regardless of what other notes are sounding.'

The choir is divided into twelve different strands, occasionally supplemented by up to six soloists, and there is a recorded tape of loon sounds that is used as a duet with one of the choir's soloists at the end of the piece. The text is made up of Ontario place names taken from the Ojibwa language, but the words are used purely for their sound rather than their meaning. On two occasions Freedman provides a list of such words from which individual singers are to choose at random. The composer has delegated to his young performers the responsibility not only for making this choice, but also for determining the order and timing of the presentation. Unconventional vocal effects are also required, including humming, speaking, *sprechstimme*, whispering, and glissandi. Even the use of traditional staff notation is largely abandoned, supplanted by graphic notation. Example 5-3 illustrates some of the innovative aspects of the score.

Example 5-3: *Keewaydin*, page 13

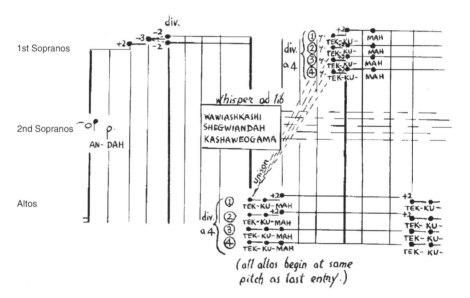

Graphic I (subtitled *Out of Silence*) was Freedman's central commitment during his term as composer-in-residence of the Toronto Symphony, and he lavished an extraordinary amount of care on its composition. He was motivated to explore new relationships, in particular those between sound and silence, between aleatoric and non-aleatoric procedures, and between electronic and conventional timbres. *Graphic I*, completed in August of 1971, is the first of Freedman's works that could justifiably be called 'avant-garde.' Though he had experimented with various innovative techniques in earlier works, he had never before mobilized them in such a comprehensive assemblage. The work is scored for full orchestra, including a large array of percussion instruments[5] as well as electronic tape. Special effects include the use of harmonics, slow glissandi, a wide variety of mutes, offstage sounds, and whistling. The prominent role of some rather exotic percussion instruments, the unconventional manner in which the conventional instruments are used, and the conspicuous presence of the electronic tape all serve to make the listener immediately aware that in this piece Freedman is exploring an entirely new sound world. The notation itself reinforces this impression, featuring open scoring and graphic symbols. Much of the score is unmeasured, and even the measured portions are largely non-pulsatile. This amorphous quality in the domain of duration is coupled with the destabilizing effect engendered by aleatoric procedures, which are present in some form in fully two-thirds of the work.

Freedman took his inspiration for *Graphic I* from both visual and literary sources. The textures of contemporary graphics evoked the images on which the work's fragmentary and delicately interwoven lines are modelled. Freedman speaks of an almost literal transfer of visual images into music. It will be recalled that early in his career the composer had written that music can only be a literal representation of 'things which have a unique *sound*,' or of 'movements which suggest *line* or *atmosphere*.' Neither criterion is valid in the case of abstract painting. Nonetheless, Freedman states clearly that he envisioned in *Graphic I* the depiction of images such as splotches of paint dripping off the page of a canvas. This change in attitude may have been facilitated by his recent embrace of graphic notation, which, in and of itself, can visually represent such an image. At Rehearsal 20 drops or spatters of paint on a canvas are suggested both in the graphic notation for the tape and in the notation of the random pizzicato repeated notes in divisi strings.[6] In example 5-4 only the viola parts are shown along with the electronic tape.

Example 5-4: *Graphic I*, Rehearsal 20–1 to 20+7, violas and electronic tape only

Even traditional notation can provide a visual stimulus. In example 5-5 the notation in the viola and cello parts does almost literally depict a quantity of paint being steadily poured onto a canvas and gradually spilling off the edge.

Example 5-5: *Graphic I*, Rehearsal 8+9 to 8+12, violas and cellos

Freedman was also influenced by literary sources in the composition of *Graphic I*. The ideas in Max Picard's book *The World of Silence*[7] inspired the composer to explore the boundary between sound and silence in a musical composition. *Graphic I* begins with a lengthy taped period of silence. Brief and extremely soft electronic episodes then begin to emerge from the silence, and recede into it again. Gradually the episodes become more intrusive, until the electronic sounds are joined almost imperceptibly by soft harmonics in the upper strings, divisi à 12. The prevailing pianissimo is abruptly shattered by a tutti sforzando, whence there is an immediate return to soft dynamics. Outbursts of this kind are rare in the piece, making them particularly conspicuous when they do occur. Another rare fortissimo augments the effect of the towering chord of forty-eight pitches spanning a four-and-a-half octave range that constitutes the piece's climactic moment at Rehearsal 22.

In general, however, volume control is managed by change in over-all density rather than change in dynamic level. There are numerous instances of a sound mass that begins as a single pitch emerging almost imperceptibly from silence. The texture then grows by gradual incre-ments to a massive structure, only to retreat once again into the silence from which it emerged. The improvisatory passage from Rehearsal 1+3 to Rehearsal 6 is a particularly extensive example of the process. Each of the string sections enters in turn with an assigned sequence of pitches. Individual players in each section are instructed to improvise on the given set of notes very softly, in a nervous irregular rhythm and at their own concept of the given tempo. The texture grows cumula-tively from a single line to a dense and chaotic sound mass in which all the strings are improvising simultaneously. The decay is accomplished by having each of the string sections fade out, one by one, until only the first violins remain. Freedman then instructs the members of that group to drop out one at a time 'beginning with the concertmaster and working back until only the last player in the section is left.'

In *Graphic I* Freedman was exploring the boundary not only between sound and silence, but tentatively that between aleatoric and non-aleatoric music as well. Beginning at Rehearsal 24 there is an extended passage of eighth-note gestures in which fully composed sections alter-nate with sections based on moving cluster chords, of the type seen ear-lier in *Klee Wyck*. (Refer again to example 5-2.) These modestly aleatoric sections reflect the fully composed sections in rhythm, length, and shape, inviting an immediate comparison, as shown in example 5-6.

At Rehearsal 19 the composer explores another interesting interface, that between electronic and conventional timbres. Percussionists are instructed to allow the taped sounds to dictate both their choice of instrument and the nature of their improvisation. The piece ends in a mirror image of the beginning, with electronic sounds gradually retreating into silence. The conductor is instructed not to put down his baton until ten seconds after the sound on the tape has disappeared.

Pan (1972) is an eclectic mixture of jazz, blues, samba, flamenco, rock, North American Indian text, and comic theatre. For the first time Freedman requires his performers actually to become actors, to move about on stage, gesture, and interact with one another. Perhaps he was

Example 5-6: *Graphic I,* Rehearsal 24+2 to 24+4

attempting to mitigate public apathy toward new music by enlivening
the work with theatrical elements and sonic novelties, and by incorporating elements from the world of popular music. The Lyric Arts Trio
constituted a particularly apt vehicle for experiments of this kind.
Founded in 1964, the group comprised flutist Robert Aitken, his wife,
pianist Marion Ross, and Freedman's wife, Mary Morrison. They soon
began to specialize in the contemporary repertoire, and by the end of
1972 had premièred about a dozen works by Canadian composers.
Although this is the first time Freedman had written specifically for
this ensemble, he had written for two of its members – Aitken and
Morrison – several years earlier, in *Toccata.* Evidently he had found
their interpretation of the innovative aspects of that work entirely satisfactory, and felt comfortable in escalating his demands on their cre-
ativity in *Pan.* Not only were the members of the trio accomplished
musicians, but they also had the gift of communicating directly and
easily with their audiences, and were collectively imbued with an
unusually keen spirit of adventure. The players are required to create a
variety of unusual sounds. The soprano uses a number of native
words, chosen by Freedman for their sound rather than their meaning.

She must not only sing, but speak, whisper, hum, shout, and click her tongue. Both the soprano and the flutist exploit the resonance of the grand piano by singing or blowing directly into the strings. The repertory of flute effects includes flutter tonguing, slapping the keys, and singing into the flute, while that of the pianist encompasses plucking and hitting the strings inside the piano, slamming the piano lid, and using props such as bottles and wire brushes. All players are required to clap, stamp their feet, and perform as comic actors as well as musicians. Just before Rehearsal 24, for example, the instructions in the score are as follows:

> After several repetitions of the last 4 bars, the flute player's foot stampings gradually get out of metre (deliberately or otherwise). The soprano tries to get him back in metre by adding the foot stamping in the right metre. But the flute ignores her and blithely goes on his way completely out of metre. In her efforts to emphasize the proper rhythm the soprano soon gets her metre bungled, at which point the pianist, who has been keeping the right time with her hand clapping, rushes over from the piano and tries to get the soprano back in metre. But the soprano refuses to be corrected and a violent argument of hand-claps and foot-stamps ensues, very quickly degenerating into utter chaos. At this point, the flute player whistles loudly, either by placing two fingers between his lips or by means of a police whistle which he has taken from his pocket. The other two stop, look at him, look at each other, and flounce haughtily back to their positions. When they are quite ready, he gives a very exaggerated upbeat with his flute to his mouth, and –

The addition of theatrical ingredients to a musical work was probably a small but natural evolutionary step for Freedman, who habitually conceived a work in dramatic terms.[8] Example 5-7 illustrates the marriage of jazz and comic elements in *Pan*.

The sketches for *Pan* are the first extant examples of the compositional modus operandi that served the composer so well through much of his career. He claims that his initial idea for a piece normally begins with a consideration of the instruments, their available timbres, and the capabilities of the performers. The first notations in his sketches for *Pan* confirm that his earliest inspiration for the piece indeed came from these sources, as evidenced by comments such as 'tongue clicks imitating pad slaps,' 'use Indian words with hard consonants,' and 'use voice to imitate brushes and guero (tata-chi-ka-pi-ka).' The precompo-

Example 5-7: *Pan,* Rehearsal 26+1 to 26+11

sitional notes continue with a list of musical elements, such as 'various 8ve passages interspersed with short glimpses of flamenco,' 'handclapping (flamenco), footstamping, finger snapping,' and '[j]azz fragments with DA-DN-DA-DN or PA-BM-PA-BM.' He describes the main theme as a 'disjunct line, syncopated,' and appends a graphic portrayal of its general shape, rhythm, and articulation. In the next stage of planning Freedman attempted to give some order to the elements he had listed. He prepared what amounts to a dramatic script for the work, describing in careful and often vivid prose the sequence of events. For example, in describing the section of *Pan* between Rehearsal 9 and Rehearsal 14 he provided the approximate shape and rhythm of the opening motive, then drafted the organization of the passage as follows: '[The motive is] treated imitatively (flute in various registers) (piano adds figures of opening to texture). All 3 instruments get busier and louder (KA-WA gradually grows to KA-WA-KA-NIKA and others) until back to blues line [Rehearsal 11] in 3 rhythms. This time dim. at end of 5th bar resolves into low flute and high piano exchanging filigree of opening very softly while voice bursts out with loud phrases into piano from time to time. (1st time moderate length, 2nd time repeat with slight variation, 3rd and 4th short, 5th long, high and loud). Last time voice interrupts and stops the others. Let echoes in piano die. Repeat with variation and let die.'

Although a comparison between the prose of the sketches for *Pan* and the final version of the score reveals that Freedman frequently departed from his initial plan, it is clear that he finds a written description a natural tool with which to organize his thoughts. He would have had considerable experience in adhering to a prepared script in writing for film and ballet, but in *Pan* he has created his own script.

Like *Graphic I* of 1971, *Graphic II* of 1972 is inspired by some of the general techniques Freedman had observed in contemporary visual arts rather than by any specific painting. He summarizes *Graphic II* as 'an aural description of abstract impressions, using a variety of lines, colours and textures.' However, only a quick glance through the score is needed to confirm that *Graphic II* constitutes a significant departure from its predecessor.

The piece is scored for string quartet, Freedman's first foray into the genre since his early *Five Pieces for String Quartet* (1949). In addition to the techniques normally expected of string players (such as the ability to produce double stopping, glissandi, natural and artificial harmonics, and pizzicato), there are several that are less commonly required in contemporaneous quartet literature, notably the ability to deal with scordatura tuning, imprecisely notated pitches, quarter-tones, and the production of vocal sounds. Each of the instruments is required to retune two of its strings: the violins each have two strings raised, the cello has two strings lowered, while the viola has one string raised and another lowered.[9] Freedman explains that this tuning was chosen because it gave him access to all twelve notes in natural harmonics. There are passages in the work in which standard noteheads are replaced by x's representing only an approximation of the pitches. In following the general contour the players are instructed to include flats, sharps, and even quarter-tones. At other points in the score the performers are also required to hum, and to speak and shout a variety of Indian words apparently selected for their sound rather than their meaning.

Freedman claims that this work marks a significant turning point in his stylistic evolution. With *Graphic II* he begins to explore the possibilities of composing with sound masses. In previous works he had relied upon short motives to imbue a work with coherence, but he now begins to see how the movement and interrelationship of large complex structures can perform the same function. *Graphic II* features both motives and sound masses, initially introduced in isolation but becoming increasingly intermingled as the work progresses.

As used by Freedman, a sound mass normally occupies a significant amount of space, both vertically and horizontally, and the space occupied is relatively saturated with sound. Freedman asserts that he doesn't necessarily require all twelve tones to create a sense of mass; he often achieves the desired effect with fewer tones. A sound mass is usually timbrally homogeneous, and is clearly delineated from adjacent material by virtue of strong contrast or punctuating elements. In addition to the now-familiar cumulative type of sound mass, there are four other distinct types in *Graphic II*:

Sound mass 1: an evolving chord (first appearance at the beginning of the piece).

Sound mass 2: a decorated chord (first appearance at Rehearsal 4+1).

Sound mass 3: layered glissandi (first appearance on page 2, system 1, measure 3).

Sound mass 4: superposed lines (first appearance at Rehearsal 3–3).

The first sound mass consists of a sustained chord whose components mutate gradually and non-synchronously. The availability of double stopping allows a dense and constantly evolving vertical conformation. This sound mass typically begins with cumulative entries and immediately begins to expand outward in a wedge shape. A dense sustained chord is the characteristic feature of the second type of sound mass also. However, this one is an octachord spanning nearly four octaves, and it does not evolve; its initial tones remain, each in turn being ornamented by adjacent tones. Covering an even larger range, the third sound mass is composed of a series of layered but non-synchronous glissandi played in harmonics. The fourth sound mass comprises a superposition of rapid, imprecisely pitched lines. The strings are divided into two pairs, the higher instruments a loose inversion of the lower. In addition to the four sound masses just described, there are two melodic motives whose narrow ranges contrast dramatically with the wide ranges encompassed by the sound masses. The first motive (heard initially at Rehearsal 2+1) is a lyrical line in irregular note values normally played by the cello, while the second motive (first heard at Rehearsal 5–1) is a busy twisting line in steady triplets, shared by all the instruments. Example 5-8 provides illustrative excerpts from the score of the four sound masses and two motives.

Example 5-8.1: *Graphic II*, sound mass 1 (begins in the last half of Rehearsal 3–1) and sound mass 4 (begins at Rehearsal 3–2)

Example 5-8.2: *Graphic II*, sound mass 2, Rehearsal 4+3 to 4+5

Example 5-8.3: *Graphic II*, sound mass 3, from system 2, page 2

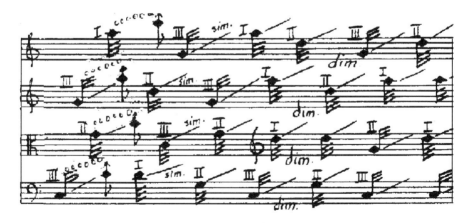

Example 5-8.4: *Graphic II*, motive 1, Rehearsal 2+9ff, cello

Example 5-8.5: *Graphic II*, motive 2, Rehearsal 5–6 to 5–2, first violin

The work is a study in stark contrasts between abutting sections, and between juxtaposed materials within a section. The formal design of the piece results from the accretion of a limited number of discrete, easily recognizable elements that are frequently varied and recombined upon restatement. For example, beginning at the top of page 7 sound mass 4 borrows the rhythm and contour of motive 2, and on page 10 sound mass 1 borrows the harmonics of sound mass 3. Similar examples can be found elsewhere in the work.

As early as 1971 Freedman had included in some of his works lists of elements – words, motives, or rhythms – that the performers were instructed to perform in whatever order they chose. However, his new method of composing in *Graphic II* is not merely an expansion of that idea to include larger musical units; it amounts to much more than a random accretion of sound masses. This piece is distinguishable in several important ways from an aleatoric piece in which the performer, provided with a list of 'sound bites,' is charged merely with determining the order in which they are to be played. An obvious difference is the progressive mutation and recombination of material that is so striking a feature of *Graphic II*. Freedman also carefully groups his material into cohesive larger sections which feature internal logic. Typically, these sections exhibit an alternation of different sound masses, with each successive statement of the same sound mass being longer than its predecessor. Developmental processes are also evident in the relationships among the sections themselves, successive sections tending to be progressively shorter than those that came before. Finally, Freedman provides a coda for the piece that effectively synthesizes, compresses, and reinterprets previously heard elements.

Although comparable techniques can be observed in the music of other composers, there is a marked similarity between Freedman's techniques in this piece and those of his erstwhile teacher, Olivier Messiaen, in pieces such as *Cantéyodjayâ* and *Vingt regards sur l'enfant Jésus*. Christianne Sawruk, in her thesis on continuity in 'Par lui' from Messiaen's *Vingt regards sur l'enfant Jésus*,[10] offers a detailed discussion of his techniques. She argues that, despite strong surface disjunctions between contiguous sections of the piece, developmental relationships exist among non-contiguous sections, creating an extended, interlocked web of continuity. As is the case with *Graphic II*, several distinct strands of evolving material can be traced.

Freedman also shares with his former teacher a passion for the visual arts. Messiaen claimed to have been deeply influenced by the painter Robert Delaunay, who in 1912–13 developed a principle that he called 'simultaneous contrast.' Delaunay perceived paintings as 'movements of coloured masses – the colour acting almost as a function of itself, by contrasts. ... Movement exists in the functions of simultaneous surfaces, with depths obtained by the creator with simultaneous contrasts.'[11] These characteristics are discernible in the work of both Freedman and Messiaen, but since Freedman claims to dislike much of Messiaen's music and to have absorbed very little from his studies with him, it would be foolish to suggest that he was deliberately emulating either Messiaen or Delaunay. In fact there is no evidence that he even knew of the work of Delaunay. However, it is clear that Freedman shared with Messiaen the conviction that techniques from the visual arts could be adapted not just to create distinctive musical lines, textures, and colours, but also to juxtapose, reorder, recombine, and subtly mutate them.

In *Tapestry*, completed in February 1973, Freedman retreats from most of the innovative techniques he had used in *Graphic II*,[12] preferring instead to make a thorough exploration of the technique of quotation. He had used the technique in a very modest way in several earlier works,[13] but in the appropriately titled *Tapestry* the texture consists almost exclusively of an intricate web of overlaid and interwoven quotations. Freedman declares the writing of *Tapestry* to have been one of the most satisfying achievements of his career because he intended the work as a kind of homage to his great idol, Johann Sebastian Bach. The sketches contain several pages of fragments extracted from a wide variety of Bach's works, including *Brandenburg Concerti*, the *Musical Offering*, the *Mass in B minor*, the *Orgelbüchlein*, the *Well-Tempered Cla-*

vier, and various cantatas. Most are easily identifiable melodic excerpts or full textures, though a few are bass lines whose origins are more obscure. Not content merely to introduce the chosen quotations in their original form, Freedman, like Bach, deliberately set himself some difficult compositional problems, the successful solution of which he considers a real intellectual accomplishment.

The quotations chosen by Freedman rarely appear unmodified and in isolation. In altering, combining, and manipulating them he emulates many of the techniques of his illustrious model. Individual quotations may be subjected to melodic changes such as segmentation, inversion, retrograde, and retrograde inversion, or undergo rhythmic changes ranging from strictly proportional augmentation and diminution to unsystematic modifications of certain note values. An individual quotation may be treated canonically, as at the opening of the work using a fragment from the first movement of Bach's *Brandenburg Concerto no. 2*, or combined with modified versions of itself, as at Rehearsal 3+4, which features layered prime, inverted, retrograde, and retrograde inverted versions of a single motive in various augmentations and diminutions. At Rehearsal 20 four different quotations are presented simultaneously, all in the key of E minor, while beginning at Rehearsal 24 several two-voiced textures extracted from different works of Bach are presented simultaneously, and in different keys.[14]

While none of the procedures described above entirely obscures the identity of the quotations, the procedures of segmentation, registral displacement, and textural dispersion, as used in *Tapestry*, can effectively render the original sources unrecognizable. In the first place, Freedman rarely segments a quotation at a natural break point in the line. Example 5-9.1 shows how segmentation and registral displacement impede identification of an excerpt from the second movement of Bach's *Brandenburg Concerto no. 4*. The eleven numbered segments are distributed among eight instruments, each of which executes many repetitions of its assigned segment(s) at irregular intervals. Despite the fact that the segments are introduced cumulatively and adhere reasonably consistently to their original ordering, octave displacement and dispersal through a dense texture reduces considerably the possibility that the listener might recognize the original source. Example 5-9.2 shows the opening portion of this passage, which contains ten of the eleven segments. The first appearance of each segment is identified in the example.

Example 5-9.1: *Tapestry,* from the sketches, segmentation and registral displacement of a fragment from the second movement of Bach's *Brandenburg Concerto no. 4*

Example 5-9.2: *Tapestry,* Rehearsal 5–6 to 5+7, first and second violins, violas, and cellos, all divisi

Even more obscure are passages such as that from Rehearsal 14 to Rehearsal 16. The quotation that provides the infrastructure for the passage is a bass line from the *St Matthew Passion* (example 5-10.1), the obscurity of which Freedman exacerbates by inverting it. Instead of dividing the inverted quotation into contiguous segments, as was the case in example 5-9.1 above, Freedman partitions it into nine over-lapped segments, some of which are also nested (example 5-10.2).

Example 5-10.1: From the sketches: original form of bass line from *St Matthew Passion*

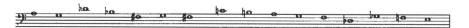

Example 5-10.2: From the sketches, bass line from example 5-10.1, inverted and segmented

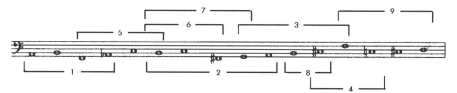

Nine instrumental layers perform all nine segments in numerical order, though each begins with a different segment. Thus the passage comprises nine successive vertical presentations of the entire quotation. The chart which illustrates the process (see next page) is slightly misleading; segments in the same column appear to occur simultaneously, but they are actually displaced, the last note of each being held while other segments in the same column take their turn to sound their assigned segment. The identity of the original quotation is further encrypted by transposition, since only the first segment in each motivic layer occurs at its original pitch level. All later segments are transposed to conform to Freedman's harmonic goal, which was to create a texture that was entirely saturated, not only with motivic segments but also with pitch classes. That is, each of the nine motivic layers is assigned a unique identifying pitch – that of the last note of its first segment – and each subsequent segment is transposed so that it ends on that pitch. The three remaining pitches necessary to complete the aggregate are allocated to three additional instruments that simply

Instrument	Segment									Assigned pitch
1st violin: div. I	9	1	2	3	4	5	6	7	8	D
1st violin: div. II	5	6	7	8	9	1	2	3	4	B
1st violin: div. III	3	4	5	6	7	8	9	1	2	F
2nd violin: div. I	Sustained E^b									E^b
2nd violin: div. II	4	5	6	7	8	9	1	2	3	C
2nd violin: div. III	7	8	9	1	2	3	4	5	6	G
Viola: div. I	8	9	1	2	3	4	5	6	7	C$^\#$
Viola: div. II	2	3	4	5	6	7	8	9	1	A
Viola: div. III	6	7	8	9	1	2	3	4	5	F$^\#$
Cello: div. I	Sustained E									E
Cello: div. II	1	2	3	4	5	6	7	8	9	A^b
Bass: div. I	Sustained A$^\#$									A$^\#$

Example 5-11: *Tapestry*, Rehearsal 14+1 to 14+6, solo first violins I, II, and III only

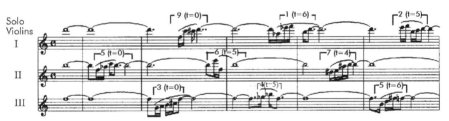

sustain their assigned pitch without involving themselves in the motivic interplay.

Example 5-11 is drawn from the opening six measures of the passage. Although only the top three layers of the texture are included, they should be sufficient to illustrate the technique.

This dense, complex texture, performed entirely by strings, is offset by various solo wind instruments rendering clear, unequivocal, and well-known quotations from other Bach sources such as 'O Sacred Head Sore Wounded,' the *Passacaglia in C minor,* and the 'Agnus Dei' from the *Mass in B minor*. While Freedman himself concedes that *Tapestry* is anomalous in his output, it remains one of his own favourite compositions.

Having composed the music for more than thirty films by the mid-1970s, Freedman had gained considerable experience in relating music and text.[15] Further evidence of his fascination with dramatic elements in music emerged in 1976. He embarked on a series of works that bear witness to his ongoing enchantment with Lewis Carroll's *Alice in Wonderland*. The inherent zaniness of the characters and story attracts him strongly and provides an ideal outlet for his whimsical sense of humour. He worked on the first two pieces in the series concurrently, completing *Alice in Wonderland* in March of 1976, and *Fragments of Alice* in April of the same year. The two works, despite their similarity in source and date of composition, are entirely different from one another stylistically. *Alice in Wonderland* is a puppet play in which all the text is spoken and prerecorded on tape, either with musical accompaniment or as pure dialogue. The pitch materials and organization are unusually diverse in this work, a number of different tone rows being employed with varying degrees of strictness. The series used in the opening gesture of this work (P0: 9 2 3 10 11 6 7 8 1 0 5 4) is also used occasionally in *Fragments of Alice* (for example, in an identical gesture at Rehearsal 47) and constitutes the only common element between the two works. In addition to tone rows, *Alice in Wonderland* features a bewildering array of scales ranging from traditional diatonic to octatonic, whole tone, and chromatic. For example, at Rehearsal 23 scales and arpeggios from five different diatonic collections are layered in a complex, polytonal texture, while at Rehearsal 7 individual layers feature whole tone, octatonic, and hybrid scales and fragments (examples 5-12.1 and 5-12.2).

Freedman exhibits a characteristically sure touch in capturing the humour and parody of Carroll's text. At Rehearsal 81, at the point where the March Hare proclaims '[I]t was at the great concert given by the Queen of Hearts, and I had to sing,' we hear a deliciously overblown parody of Wagnerian operatic style (example 5-13) which culminates at Rehearsal 83–10 with an equally exaggerated impersonation of the ending of Beethoven's *Symphony no. 5*. In the intervening passage (beginning at Rehearsal 82) Freedman interjects a travesty of a traditional nursery tune, now rendered as 'Twinkle Twinkle little bat, How I wonder what you're at!'

Example 5-12.1: *Alice in Wonderland*, Rehearsal 23+1 to 23+3

Example 5-12.2: *Alice in Wonderland*, Rehearsal 7+1 to 7+6

Example 5-13: *Alice in Wonderland*, Rehearsal 81+1 to 81+6

Fragments of Alice, on the other hand, is a chamber work for a medium-sized instrumental group and three singers who, as the name of the piece suggests, perform short, unrelated fragments from Carroll's text. Freed from the necessity of adhering to a story line, Freedman creates a far less structured score and a highly linear approach to texture. Frequently, each part is assigned its own small collection of pitches whose deployment is either fully prescribed or permitted a degree of latitude, but in either case the essential ingredient of the line is the irregular repetition of a limited number of pitches. For example, the opening of the work, based on the passage 'Begin at the beginning and go on until you come to the end. Then stop,' consists of twelve discrete layers, each comprising two or three pitches. Following the peremptory opening chord ('Begin!'), the layers enter cumulatively, each repeating its assigned pitches at irregular intervals punctuated with rests. The confusion inherent in this texture mirrors the mixed message being sent out by the singers, one of whom sings 'begin,' another 'stop,' and the third 'go on.' Although the passage is fully written out, the effect is remarkably aleatoric.

The aleatoric techniques seen in *Tsolum Summer* (1976) constitute, for Freedman, the natural limits of this form of expression. The ubiquity and audacity of the graphic notation in this work are unique in his output, and symbolize the unprecedented degree of artistic licence he grants his performers. Rhythm is virtually never represented in conventional notation; instead, noteheads are positioned on the horizontal axis to indicate points of attack, often with horizontal lines appended to indicate duration. Pitch, on the other hand, is represented precisely on the vertical axis for approximately half the piece, while the remainder features an imaginative collection of freehand lines to portray the effect he wishes to achieve. Example 5-14 is a representative excerpt from the score.

Example 5-14: *Tsolum Summer*, Rehearsal 8–1

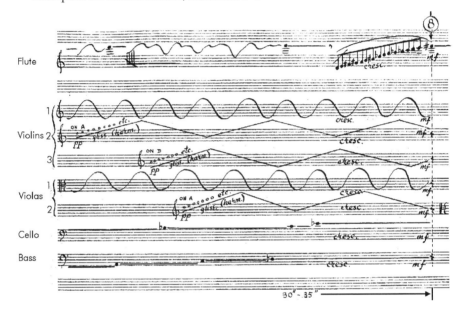

The sketches for *Tsolum Summer* comprise both the musical materials and a clear description of the manner in which they are to be used. Interestingly, while much of the musical material is fully and conventionally notated in the sketches, it is rendered in imprecise graphic notation in the score. Freedman obviously had a clear image of the general effect he wished to create, but deliberately rendered his ideas ambiguously in the score in order to achieve the serendipitous results made possible by performer input. For Freedman, aleatoric procedures were never an easy mechanism for avoiding the rigours of traditional composition, much less an exercise in drawing pretty pictures. He finds it difficult to identify with the Cageian philosophy of art as a slice of life. Rather, he subscribes to the Boethian philosophy of art as a rational and intellectual phenomenon that must contain and exhibit craft. Freedman does not wish to abdicate what he views as his responsibility as a composer by delegating too many compositional decisions to the performers.

Like most of the other works examined in this chapter, the last work, *The Explainer* of 1976, is an experiment, in this case in the art of musical satire. The theatrical antics of the performers that were seen earlier in such works as *Pan* are now augmented with the pompous declamations of a narrator. The text for *The Explainer* was taken directly from program notes written by composers about their own music. Freedman, appalled at their pretentiousness and excessive use of jargon, decided to compile some of the more outrageous phrases into a wholly irreverent script. He claims that the target of his sarcasm was not musicologists or music critics, but his fellow composers, who he believes often take themselves too seriously.

The narrator, or 'Explainer,' is ostensibly analysing a composition for the edification of the audience. He begins by describing the four kinds of sound 'raw materials' that are used in the work. Each is then demonstrated, tongue-in-cheek, by the performers (example 5-15).

Another extract from the text (pages 10–11) will be sufficient to give the reader the full flavour of Freedman's sarcasm. The narrator arrogantly proclaims: 'The simple phrase, built on a diatonic progression of 2nds, grinding itself in the muddy blotch of sound and dying at the end on an open 5th, is based on a simultaneity that adds to itself and gradually completes the chromatic scale. One hears this phrase as intended archaization – intended, because timeless truth rendered in a manner which so contrasts with the musical content, gains in substance a broad sense of objectified generalization, which is quasi-imitationally changeable within the texture.' The performers, who have been listening incredulously to this nonsense, respond with a loud, derisive raspberry.

Just as *Tsolum Summer* of 1976 represents the outer limits of Freedman's experiments with aleatoric procedures, so *The Explainer* of the same year delineates the boundaries of his exploration into the realm of comic musical satire. Although both aleatoric procedures and dramatic humour remain integral parts of his craft, they are employed more conservatively after 1976.

Example 5-15: *The Explainer*, Rehearsal 5ff

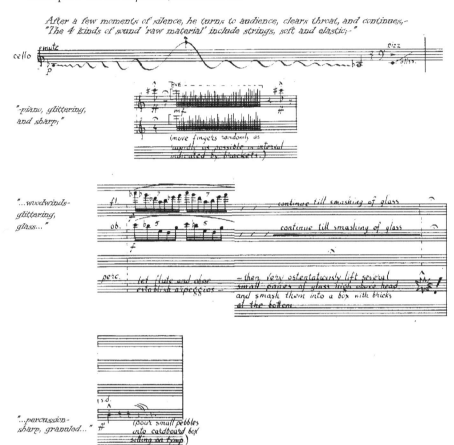

Chapter Six

The Mature Stylistic Spectrum
(1977 to the Present)

By 1977 Freedman was gaining increasing recognition as a composer, both in Canada and abroad. A CBC radio documentary dedicated entirely to his work was prepared by Norma Beecroft and broadcast on the thirteenth of September 1977. His international reputation was growing also, as evidenced by the performance in that same year of a number of his pieces, including *Tangents, Brass Quintet,* and *Keewaydin* at the CAPAC Festival in Bonn, Germany. However, 1977 was not chosen as the starting point for this chapter because that year was distinguished by any cataclysmic event or dramatic stylistic change. Rather, 1977 marks a point in Freedman's development at which the wholesale experimentation with new techniques, new genres, and new concatenations of different techniques or idioms has largely come to an end. This is not to say that his style in this final period has become homogeneous. It is simply that his mastery of individual techniques and stylistic idioms has matured sufficiently that he can summon any of them, for whatever purpose and in whatever combinations, in full confidence of their effect and interaction. He can use them individually when the character of a piece demands it, or combine any number of them seamlessly into a cohesive composition. Some works written during this period are wholly or largely oriented toward a particular style, from pop or jazz at one end of the spectrum to serious concert music at the opposite end. Other works exhibit a skilful blend of different styles, notably a melding of serious and jazz traditions, the relative proportions of each in a given work determining its stylistic bias.

In the years following 1977, Freedman's compositional methods exhibit only a modest amount of growth or change, as compared with the rapid pace of development in earlier periods. Paradoxically, his output becomes increasingly eclectic as he grows more confident in his ability to adapt his methods to a broad spectrum of genres and styles. Even a cursory glance at his List of Works composed since 1977 will reveal the heterogeneity of his output, which includes such diverse genres and styles as a concerto grosso, a pop opera, a symphony, a ballet based on Venezuelan dance tunes, a jazz concerto, a work for four choirs and orchestra, one for viola, percussion, and synthesizer, and even a 'kitchen' cantata.

In previous chapters it has been possible to discuss in some detail a large proportion of the works composed during the period under discussion. However, the volume of work produced by Freedman in the time period covered by the current chapter is truly prodigious. Although almost all of the works are solidly crafted and worthy of discussion, comprehensive coverage of such an abundant output is obviously impossible in the present context. Given the focus of the study on stylistic evolution, and taking into account the relative stability of Freedman's stylistic spectrum after 1977, it has seemed reasonable to cover a much smaller proportion of his output in this chapter. This decision has necessarily resulted in the exclusion of a number of major and entirely worthy works from detailed study. On the other hand, several smaller works have been singled out for close analysis on the grounds that they are representative of a particular genre or exhibit stylistically important developments.

Perhaps the most significant development after 1977 has occurred in the basic materials of Freedman's tonal language. While serialism has remained an important resource, much of his writing features a free chromaticism with a noticeable tendency toward aggregate completion. He has also employed a wide variety of tonal resources in response to the exigencies of the particular piece at hand. His more traditional source materials have included modal scales (as in the 1977 film/television soundtrack *1847*), major and minor scales (in his pop- or folk-oriented works such as *Abracadabra* and *Blue ... Green ... White*), whole tone scales (in the 1978 work *November*, for example), octatonic scales (in *Nocturne III, Royal Flush*, and others), and pentatonic scales (in *Touchings* of 1989). However, after 1993 or so Freedman regularly supplemented his tonal language with two new scales derived from a favourite jazz chord. He describes this new language as more 'North American' and more 'integrated,' by which he means that the jazz-derived scales he had employed sporadically and tentatively prior to that time had now become significant pitch resources in both linear and vertical dimensions.[1]

Jazz elements remain an important component of Freedman's style throughout the period. Melodic, harmonic, and rhythmic jazz idioms occur frequently, though with considerable variety in their levels of perceptibility. Although there is some evidence of jazz in almost every work he has written in this period, its prevalence varies between two extremes of a broad spectrum. At one extreme are pieces like *Monday Gig* (1978) that are strongly rooted in jazz from their initial conception, a circumstance in which the preponderance of jazz elements is hardly surprising. At the other extreme are pieces of a solemn nature, such as *Epitaph for Igor Stravinsky* (also written in 1978), in which the use of jazz idioms is virtually non-existent. Between these two extremes lies the bulk of his output, in which jazz and serious elements coexist in a delicate balance. Prior to 1993, jazz elements in Freedman's writing often seemed to be adjunctive rather than integral parts of the musical fabric. However, after 1993 his use of jazz is inherent in the tonal language itself. His jazz-derived scales become a key component of works in a wide variety of styles, though it is important to note that their use often yields results that are not jazzy in the least.

His fascination with folk materials endures as an important influence on his style to this day. Idioms derived from folk songs and dances manifest themselves in a variety of ways, ranging from the inclusion of authentic folk materials within an otherwise original composition to the creation of pseudo-folk materials based on existing models.

The mature Freedman has also become increasingly fascinated with texture, in particular with large, dense sound masses. He is interested not only in the timbre of these textural groups, but also in the processes by which they are created, developed, and dissipated. An examination of his more recent compositions reveals a pronounced increase in both the prevalence and contiguity of these sound masses.

In consultation with Freedman, I have chosen for detailed discussion eight works, written from 1977 to 1997, that we agree are representative of a certain genre or aspect of his style, or embody a significant stylistic development. In chronological order these works are *Celebration* (1977), *Caper* (1978), *Abracadabra* (1979), *Nocturne III* (1980), *Royal Flush* (1981), *Symphony no. 3* (1983), *Oiseaux exotiques* (1984), and *Borealis* (1997).

Celebration (1977) was commissioned by the CBC on the occasion of saxophonist Gerry Mulligan's fiftieth birthday. This large concerto is a jazz-oriented work for saxophone and full symphony orchestra. While embracing some of the principles of mainstream serious music, *Celebration* gives full expression to Freedman's predilection for jazz. The work could be described as 'third stream,' provided the term is used in a broad sense to denote a conflation of idioms typically associated with any type of jazz and those typically associated with the European art music tradition.[2] The score calls for a wealth of instruments commonly associated with jazz. Besides the solo soprano and baritone saxophones there is a wide variety of percussion instruments, many of which, like the jazz set, are not part of the normal complement of orchestral instruments. The jazz-based genesis of *Celebration* is also evident in its melodic, rhythmic, and harmonic material, its use of typical features such as walking pizzicato bass lines, and its emphasis on improvisation. Virtually all of the thematic material features idioms typically found in jazz. An underpinning of tertian-based chords is very common, especially to support improvisation. Both sketches and score abound with chord symbols such as E^9, $C^{13\ b5}$, and A major[7]. Although the relationship among successive chords is not traditionally functional, there is a noticeable preponderance of third relation among successive chord roots. At the other end of the spectrum, the influence of serious art music is manifest in *Celebration* in the liberal use of structured, multilayered counterpoint, systematically assembled sound masses, and highly organized formal structures.

Freedman had written several jazz-oriented works earlier in his career, notably *Scenario* (1970) and *Pan* (1972). *Pan* was written for a small chamber group and was clearly a lightweight, even comic work, but *Scenario* was a true precursor of *Celebration* in that it attempted to integrate classical idioms within a jazz-oriented, large-scale, serious work for full orchestra. Both *Scenario* and *Celebration* are essentially jazz pieces, and thus fundamentally different from other pieces that are merely flavoured with jazz. The creative process in these and a few similar works actually begins with and emanates directly from jazz.[3] A comparison between *Scenario* and *Celebration* points up the distance Freedman has travelled in grafting classical idioms onto a jazz-based work. In both compositions one can trace a large variety of diverse elements, but in *Celebration* they interact more convincingly than is the case in *Scenario*. The use of improvisation in *Celebration* is considerably less pervasive, and more carefully regulated when it does occur. In *Scenario* Freedman frequently directs a group of instruments to improvise simultaneously, imposing few restrictions on the nature of the material or the method of improvisation. However, in *Celebration* he restricts improvisation to the solo saxophone and percussion instruments, and usually controls the outcome by giving clear directions. Further, he provides clear harmonic underpinnings for most of the improvisatory sections in *Celebration*, and often adds one or more layers of written-out parts from which, clearly, the improviser is intended to draw inspiration. In *Scenario* one gets the impression that Freedman is attempting to maximize diversity and to bring as many elements as possible into close juxtaposition. In *Celebration* the integration is more complete, and the disparate components are blended together more subtly.

The first use of improvisation in the piece occurs within a symmetrically structured section from Rehearsal 13 to 15. The thirty-two measures are divided into four eight-measure segments, the first and third of which feature identical tertian chordal successions. The second eight-measure section is shown in example 6-1. The solo saxophone is directed to improvise, making liberal use of the contour and rhythm of three motives that had been introduced singly earlier on. Freedman reinforces the connection by writing out the motives in full for the non-improvising instruments. Two of the motives are shown in the example, labelled 'a' and 'b.' The chordal progression supplied for the improvising saxophone is echoed in the running pizzicato line in the string basses and the motivic gestures in the flutes and first horn. The trombones and third horns perform a supporting role by highlighting the chordal roots in descending thirds.

Example 6-1: *Celebration*, Rehearsal 13+9 to 13+16

A particularly revealing example of the juxtaposition between jazz and classical orientations can be found between Rehearsal 13 and

Rehearsal 18. With the exception of two brief orchestral interruptions, the lengthy section from Rehearsal 13 to Rehearsal 16 had focused on the saxophone's improvisation on the three assigned motives, supported by typical jazz rhythms in the percussion instruments and enhanced by occasional motivic gestures in the other instruments. In an abrupt change of mood at Rehearsal 16, the orchestral instruments provide an entirely new perspective on the same motivic materials. The improvisatory treatment is now supplanted by a lengthy, carefully structured contrapuntal interplay on the same motives. For practical reasons the illustrative excerpt provided in example 6-2 has been condensed from the original sixteen instrumental lines to five staves. The full texture involves considerably more motivic interplay among the various instruments than is evident in the example. The seven-measure excerpt chosen from this extended contrapuntal section focuses on motives 'a' and 'b,' both having undergone considerable evolution. The arpeggiated descent followed by a reverse in direction that characterized the original form of motive 'a' is evident in the example (measure 6, third stave), but the motive also appears in augmentation and inverted (measures 5 to 6, second stave), and in retrograde (opening five notes of the first stave). The oscillating neighbour motion that initiated the early statements of motive 'b' occurs in this example in measure 3, third stave and measure 7, second stave. The entire twenty-nine-measure contrapuntal section is complex, carefully structured, and has none of the improvisatory character of jazz.

Example 6-2: *Celebration*, Rehearsal 16+1 to 16+7

Large, systematically assembled, divisi string sound masses find an unlikely home within this jazz-based work as well. The most extensive of these passages in *Celebration* is found from Rehearsal 21–6 to Rehearsal 24, during which section the string players are divided into twenty-six parts, some of which occasionally employ double stopping to further fragment the texture. The string players enter cumulatively, each performing one or more successive notes from a descending sequence of pitches and sustaining the final pitch for a variable length of time. The sequence of pitches, B^{b6} A^{b6} F^6 E^6 $D^{\#6}$ $C^{\#6}$ B^5 A^5 G^5 $F^{\#5}$ D^5 C^5 / B^{b4} G^4 $F^{\#4}$ F^4 E^{b4} $C^{\#4}$ B^3 A^3 $G^{\#3}$ E^3 D^3 C^3 / B^{b2} G^2 $F^{\#2}$ F^2, is distinguished by the completion of the aggregate (indicated by the forward slashes) before any pc is repeated. Even before the entire sequence of pitches has been heard, the texture begins gradually to erode from the top, beginning with the first element of the sequence, B^{b6}, and proceeding in order downward to F^4. The order in which the individual parts drop out is determined by the position of their final sustained tone in the above sequence of pitches. The lowest twelve parts then sustain and embellish their final notes with trills, assuming in this middle section the role of accompaniment, whereupon the entire process is reversed. That is, the lower twelve parts drop out one at a time, beginning with the lowest. Overlapping with this process is the cumulative addition of the upper parts, from lowest to highest. Once again, the aggregate is completed before any pc in the sequence is repeated. The texture gradually erodes until only the original high B^b remains. Rendered in a graphic format, the string parts would form a symmetrical shape that begins with a single high starting point, thickens as it undulates downward toward a lengthy static mass, then reverses the process to end exactly where it began. Example 6-3 presents the sixth through twentieth measures of this sixty-bar passage.

The moment the active development of this sound mass is suspended midway in the process in favour of a sustained chord, a very different mood emerges. The orientation shifts toward the jazz end of the spectrum when a rapid octatonic anacrusis introduces a languid, almost elegiac melody in the saxophone, as illustrated in example 6-4.[4]

Highly organized formal structures are typical of *Celebration*. The sketches set out the order, duration (in minutes and seconds), and specific functions of sections, using conventional terms such as 'introductory,' 'thematic,' and 'bridge.' Freedman's carefully structured formal design is also evident in the definition of the boundaries of many sections by means of similar opening and closing gestures. The above

Example 6-3: *Celebration*, Rehearsal 21–1 to 21+14, divisi strings

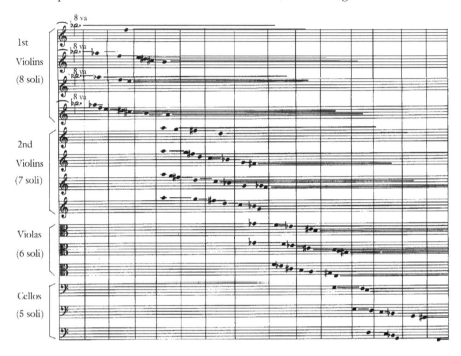

Example 6-4: *Celebration*, Rehearsal 22+1 to 22+10, saxophone and divisi violas and cellos

description of a divisi string sound mass (Rehearsal 21–6 to 24) demonstrates how large formal sections can be framed by similar material.

The next piece to be discussed provides a total contrast with *Celebration*. *Caper* (1978) is a short one-movement work for solo tuba, and a fine example of Freedman's puckish sense of humour and flair for theatrics. The work was commissioned by tuba player Dennis Miller, with the assistance of the Canada Council. When the composition was completed Miller refused to perform it, apparently believing that Freedman was deliberately making fun of him. It was subsequently successfully performed by other tuba players who claim to have thoroughly enjoyed the experience. However, Freedman was disappointed that the person for whom the work was originally composed was unwilling to make the attempt.[5]

While this piece is a deliberate exploitation of the comic potential of the tuba, its beginning is deceptively tame and conventional. The opening rising melodic gesture ('a') embodies Freedman's trademark pc set class 3-5 (016) in typical open arrangement. This is followed immediately by a more rapid gesture ('b'), which incorporates another of Freedman's favoured intervallic collections, pc set class 3-8 (026), as a subset. (See example 6-5.1, below.) This material is developed in a conventional manner for the entire first page, closure of this section of the piece being effected by a lengthy silence. The use of silence in this piece is interesting. In part, of course, it is introduced in order to allow the player of this capacious instrument to replenish his air supply, but often rests are strategically placed in order to heighten a sense of comedy as well. For example, the full bar of silence at the end of the first page serves not only to set apart the opening section of the A B A[1] design, but also sets the stage for the entirely unexpected, raucous double forte glissando that follows at the top of the second page. Until this point there had been no theatrics. Now, the player is called upon to become an actor as well as a musician. His first foray into the realm of theatre takes the form of a measure of silence in which he looks to left and right before embarking abruptly on the first sixteenth-note passage of the piece. The player is very shortly required to fulfil increasingly immoderate and outrageous instructions such as 'Slowly and stealthily, peek around rim into the bell. Then, with a fiendish, Harpo Marx grin, look to r. and l., then slowly move back to mouthpiece,' and, later, 'Sing in high, loud falsetto. React with expression of amazement ("Is this sound coming out of me"?), changing to one of self-satisfied delight.' In addition to all these theatrics, the score calls for a number of unconventional sounds such as rattling of valves, slapping of tuba, tapping with finger-nails, and humming or singing while playing.

In section A^1 the material from the opening section returns, now extended from seven bars to eleven and imbued with a comedic aspect by means of foot stamps, shouts, and slaps. A comparison of example 6-5.2 with example 6-5.1 will point up the transformation.

Example 6-5.1: *Caper*, page 1, measures 1 to 7

Example 6-5.2: *Caper*, page 4, measures 29 to 39

⊠ = stamp foot   ⤬ = slap tuba   ⊓ = shout

At the end of the final section, the comedic aspect of the piece reaches its apex. The player is instructed to perform a 'mishmash of notes, shouts, slaps, and stamps, the arpeggio figures rising higher and higher (don't worry about cracking a few notes – the more harassed the better), the entire passage becoming more and more frantic (with facial expression to match) until abrupt cutoff.' Freedman represents the effect graphically, as shown in example 6-6.

Example 6-6: *Caper*, page 5, measure 24

The work ends with a glissando in which the player is to '[h]alf rise out of chair, take a deep breath as though about to scream, hold for 2–3 seconds. Then – (Remove and reverse mouthpiece surreptitiously during the action described above.) – subside onto chair, almost simultaneously blow through stem (like a great sigh), and collapse over tuba.' This is vintage Freedman humour, but clearly, *Caper* is not a piece for the inhibited player.

The next piece to be discussed was selected because it represents the ultimate affirmation of Freedman's long-repressed interest in the idiom of pop, as opposed to jazz. *Abracadabra*, completed in March of 1979, is a one-act comic opera on a wonderfully wacky libretto by Mavor Moore. The principal characters are Dodo, an unemployed folksinger; Dodo's mother, a somewhat sleazy, though hard-nosed cocktail waitress; the boss, a shady promoter of recordings; Nona, the boss's daughter; and the fixer, strong-arm man for the boss. Briefly, the plot is as follows: Dodo's mother, frustrated with Dodo's indigence, pawns his beloved guitar and instructs him to earn a living as an astrologist instead. Though he is entirely unschooled in astrology, Dodo, quite by accident, makes various predictions that turn out to be true. For example, he exclaims 'fat chance' when asked if he knows which horse will win at the races that day, and, of course, 'Fat Chance' turns out to be the winner. The boss hears about Dodo's alleged astrological abilities and orders him to discover who has stolen his monthly take from disk jockeys across the country. The boss's fixer and his friends, enforcers I and II, threaten Dodo with unimaginable consequences should he fail to achieve satisfactory results. Terrified, Dodo asks for four hours to come up with the answer. At the end of each hour Dodo makes an innocent comment that turns out to be clairvoyant. The thieves, among whom are actually the fixer and enforcers I and II, overhear the comments and believe their crimes have been discovered by Dodo. Fearful that he will denounce them to the boss, the scoundrels readily agree to return the stolen loot. In gratitude for Dodo's success in recovering the money, the boss offers him a job with his firm. Dodo refuses, asking instead for the hand of Nona, the boss's daughter. All ends happily, with Dodo and Nona pledging their eternal love, and the boss rejoicing in the return of his loot. Even the mother and fixer are happy, having stealthily pocketed a portion of the loot for themselves.

This is a quite conventional number opera. The work features thirteen singer/actors and a moderate-sized instrumental ensemble consisting of flute, clarinet, saxophones (alto, tenor, and baritone), two trumpets, two trombones, tuba, jazz set, amplified guitar, and double bass. A brief opening instrumental prelude leads seamlessly into a lengthy full vocal ensemble. There follows a succession of songs (solos, duos, and trios) interspersed with accompanied spoken dialogue. The opera culminates as it began, with a full vocal ensemble.

'Pure pop' is the way Freedman describes the songs in this opera, and the pop genealogy of the songs is clearly evident. Each song establishes and maintains a consistent mood. Structurally, most songs are strophic, with each strophe either an exact or slightly modified musical repetition of the first. Many of the strophes conform to conventional norms of twelve or sixteen measures, often subdivided into groups of four. However, Freedman frequently thwarts any sense of inevitability engendered by this time-honoured formula by separating successive verses with spoken dialogue and action. Harmonically, he relies heavily on tertian-based chords, usually sevenths or ninths. The most prevalent relationship among successive chordal roots is the perfect fifth, and there is a strong sense of tonal centre, with many songs actually provided with key signatures. Occasionally, the melody note that appears with a chord can be interpreted only with difficulty as a member of that chord. For example, in the fourth measure of the song *My Fantasy* (example 6-7.1) the pitch C in the vocal line (Rehearsal 12+4) could perhaps be interpreted as an added eleventh to the Gm^7 chord in the guitar, but it is more likely to be heard as a free, non-chord tone. Melodic rhythms, though generally uncomplicated and square, are frequently enlivened by written-out syncopation or an instruction to the performer to sing freely within the beat. Further interest is provided by the instrumental accompaniment, which typically furnishes a contrapuntal counterfoil as well as harmonic underpinning for the melodic line or spoken dialogue.

Freedman's music aptly depicts both the action of the plot and the personality of each character. Two melodies are associated with the impractical Dodo. In *My Fantasy*, first heard in Scene I, Dodo expresses his yearning for love by crooning a slow, dreamy melody while accompanying himself with strummed guitar chords (example 6-7.1). This song, revisited a number of times during the opera, is shared by Nona, who also yearns for a lover. The other song associated with Dodo is *Your Future*, which first appears in Scene III. The song represents Dodo's soulful attempt to sell his astrological 'expertise' to passers-by. Built over a low pedal point, the languid phrases end in a drooping figure, perhaps emblematic of Dodo's lack of conviction in his ability as an astrologer (example 6-7.2). Dodo's mother, unlike her unworldly son, speaks her mind in a brassy, aggressive, slangy idiom enhanced by a jazz-rock beat (example 6-7.3). Like *My Fantasy* and *Your Future*, this song is a recurrent element in the opera. The fixer exudes a suitably sinister air when threatening Dodo. In this case, it is the accompaniment as much as the melody that provides the atmosphere of foreboding (example 6-7.4). Still another set of character traits is evident in the boss, whose arrogance and pomposity are wonderfully portrayed by the four-square rhythm of the melody, reinforced by solemn triadic chords in the low brass (example 6-7.5).

Example 6-7.1: *Abracadabra*, Rehearsal 12+1 to 12+8

Example 6-7.2: *Abracadabra*, Rehearsal 27–9 to 27+7

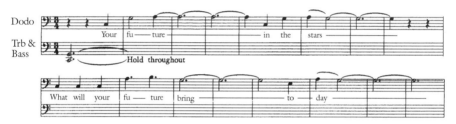

Example 6-7.3: *Abracadabra*, Rehearsal 17+5 to 17+9

Mother's text: Will ya get it thru your ever-lo-vin' head that life is just a lou-sy rat race? It's a rat race ! To stay a-live —

Example 6-7.4: *Abracadabra*, Rehearsal 36+4 to 36+11

Example 6-7.5: *Abracadabra*, Rehearsal 69+1 to 69+4

Freedman occasionally uses motifs associated with the various characters in order to provide another level of meaning to the surface action. For example, in Scene 6 (page 64, measures 4 to 6), while Nona innocently hums the *My Fantasy* tune, the alto saxophone softly sounds a version of the opening motive from the fixer's song, an ominous warning that the fixer's appearance on the scene is imminent. The ensuing spoken altercation between Nona and the fixer is enhanced by an instrumental argument based on their respective motives.

Although Freedman only rarely refers in a direct fashion to his early fascination with pop, in *Abracadabra* he shows himself entirely at ease in the idiom. The audience can never forget, however, that they are listening to the music of a classically trained composer. The potential for banality, given the nature of the melodic lines, is never realized, thanks to the active participation of the instrumental accompaniment in portraying character, developing action, and enhancing mood.

In 1980 Freedman's growing reputation as a composer was acknowledged by the Canadian Music Council when it bestowed upon him the prestigious title of Composer of the Year. This was also the year in which the Canadian Broadcasting Corporation issued a boxed set of six LPs devoted exclusively to his music as part of its Anthology of Canadian Music. Meanwhile, Freedman's work on new compositions continued unabated. *Nocturne III*, composed during that year, was commissioned by the Bach-Elgar Choral Society for its seventy-fifth anniversary season.

Freedman asserts that *Nocturne III* was inspired to some degree by techniques used much earlier in *Keewaydin*. Certainly the two works share an interest in divisi choral textures to create dense clusters of sound. The texts in both works feature words and syllables chosen for their sound rather than for their meaning. The scope and type of improvisation expected of the choir are similar as well, with each singer in both pieces given a choice of a particular word from a list, or a particular starting pitch from within a range of pitches. Otherwise, however, the works are totally dissimilar. *Nocturne III* is scored for a full adult choir and a traditional symphony orchestra in which the strings frequently divide into multiple parts and employ mutes and harmonics. The percussion instruments, which include harp, glockenspiel, and vibraphone, provide a tranquil and understated backdrop for the lush, romantic principal theme. Several versions of this theme are used in the work, including one dubbed by Freedman in his sketches as the 'love version.' The other important melodic material is an English horn theme which he subtitles 'shepherd pipe theme' in the sketches. Distinctive features render each theme easily recognizable despite considerable modifications in their successive appearances. Another unifying element is the frequently recurring slow undulation of melodic seconds with which the work opens.

Nocturne III is a good exemplar of Freedman's approach to pitch organization in a serious concert work at this stage in his career. An interest in rigorous methods of pitch control manifests itself from time to time, either in the sketches or in the final score. For example, at Rehearsal 14 in the final score he begins with an explosion of non-rhythmicized pitches by xylophone, vibraphone, glockenspiel, and harp. The sketches show that originally he intended each instrument to use a different form (either P, R, I, or RI) of a single twelve-tone row as the basis for this passage, but final revisions rendered the version in the score much less structured.

On another occasion revision had precisely the opposite effect. Examples 6-8.1 and 6-8.2 provide a comparison between the 'love version' of the principal theme (as it appears in the violins at Rehearsal 7) with Freedman's original sketch for it (opening entry, first page of sketches). The rhythm and the melodic contour are retained and several of the most prominent pitches and intervals remain in the same relative position in the two versions, but many pitches have been altered in the ultimate realization. Whereas in his initial sketch he appears to have been primarily interested in melodic shape and characteristic intervals, in his final version he concerns himself with total pitch content as well. In the sketch the first twelve melodic pitches comprise only six unique pitch classes, while in the final version each succession of twelve melodic pitches defines the aggregate. Clearly, completion of the total chromatic was a prime concern for Freedman when making these revisions.

Example 6-8.1: *Nocturne III*, Sketches, page 1, first line

Example 6-8.2: *Nocturne III*, Rehearsal 7+1 to 7+7, first violins

Elsewhere in the work, Freedman makes use of an octatonic rather than a twelve-tone scale. At Rehearsal 2 there is a carefully planned expansion from the unison by the choir, its SATB components each divisi à 3. The initial pitch B^{b3} is sustained as the nexus from which the remaining pitches fan out in both directions. Successive pitches above the initial B^{b3} are B^3 $C^{\#4}$ D^4 / E^4 F^4 G^4 A^{b4} // B^{b4} B^4 $C^{\#5}$ D^5 E^5 F^5 G^5, while those below it are A^{b3} G^3 F^3 E^3, reversing the pitch classes of the second segment above. The impact of this octatonic linear presentation is reinforced by its verticalization at the culmination of the passage (example 6-9).

Example 6-9: *Nocturne III*, Rehearsal 2+1 to 2+7, choir

The sketches reveal an interesting point about the generation of this passage. Freedman did not start out with an octatonic scale; instead, he began with two septatonic scales which he superposed and aligned as follows:

$B^{\#}$	$C^{\#}$	D	E^b	F	G	$A^{\#}$
B	$C^{\#}$	D	E	F	$G^{\#}$	$A^{\#}$

The two scales between them comprise ten unique pcs, with $F^{\#}$ and A excluded. However, in working with the material, he chose ultimately to combine the two into one octatonic scale, excluding E^b and $B^{\#}$ along with the $F^{\#}$ and A.

In fact, systematic approaches to pitch organization such as those described above occur only sporadically in *Nocturne III*, and indeed in most of Freedman's works in this period. While the active participation of all twelve pitch classes remains an overall goal, Freedman resorts only intermittently to a rigorous process governing their deployment. His interest is normally focused on timbre, on motivic development, and on the movement of large sound masses rather than on the precise choice and ordering of pitch.

Nocturne III is an important representation of Freedman's methods of handling dense, untexted choral textures. One such instance was illustrated in example 6-9, above. Another interesting texture occurs at Rehearsal 8+4 (example 6-10). Sopranos, tenors, and violins perform a version of the principal theme in triple octaves, but these lines are supported by a thickened version of the theme in the altos and basses. Freedman accomplishes this by writing the same tune approximately a third lower, and thickening each constituent tone with a cluster extending a fifth below it. Each singer in the alto and bass sections is assigned an approximate position (high, middle, or low) within the first cluster, and sings an approximation of the melody thereafter, retaining an analogous position within succeeding clusters. Because of its isolation in octaves at the top of the texture, the tune will be clearly heard, but the accompaniment will have the effect of a dense, fuzzy reflection of the original.

Example 6-10: *Nocturne III*, Rehearsal 8+4 to 8+8, choir and violins

Nocturne III also illustrates Freedman's ability to commingle an eclectic variety of styles and procedures into an effective mosaic. For example, at Rehearsal 14 a chaotic flurry of rapid, superposed lines in xylophone, vibraphone, glockenspiel, and harp forms the unlikely introduction to an entirely orthodox five-voice fugato based on the incipit of the 'shepherd pipe' theme. This almost archaic instrumental fugato is jolted to a sudden stop by a unison stage whisper of the word 'Tsi-a-na-na-nish,' the final 'sh' of which is sustained. An aleatoric section follows, featuring spoken words such as 'Te-shu-na-sa,' 'Ka-sha-we-o-sa-na,' 'O-chi-pi-ni-ka-yiss,' and 'Sa-ga-na-cha.' The singers are instructed to choose phrases at random from a list and whisper them excitedly, all hard consonants to be spat out explosively. The contrast between the conventional fugato section and the sections that frame it could hardly be more striking.

A similar dramatic contrast of juxtaposed material occurs at the end of the piece, following Rehearsal 19. This time the contrast occurs between superposed textural layers rather than between successive sections. The choir begins an extended statement of the principal theme in unison, but quickly thickens to a four-part homophonic chordal texture. Toward the close of the section, this very conventional textural layer is joined by a sharply contrasting layer featuring rapid reiterations of seven or eight ordered pitches in the flute, clarinet, and percussion along with undulating glissandi in the harp.

There follows a section without precedent anywhere else in the piece. Virtually all of the melodic material after Rehearsal 21 emanates from the slowly undulating melodic seconds that had opened the work and formed a recurrent element thereafter. Beginning at Rehearsal 21 the strings project this material as a pianissimo backdrop to a dialogue between three groups of brass instruments, two of which are offstage. Although the motives of the brass groups are rhythmically distinctive, they each draw upon the undulating seconds for their incipit. Four horns initiate the dialogue with a short homorhythmic call. Immediately three muted trumpets respond from offstage with their own chordal gesture, now at a much more rapid tempo. Following a pause, three trombones join the conversation, which rapidly becomes an argument between the two sets of offstage instruments. Against the peaceful and static backdrop of the strings the offstage trumpets and trombones become increasingly agitated, interrupting one another in a random and disjointed manner. To accomplish this end Freedman instructs the offstage brass groups not to try to synchronize either with one another or with the orchestra. When the argument offstage eventually dies away, the horns reassert themselves with several statements of their own motive. The interval of a second continues to propel the action until the end of the piece. The choir alludes to that interval when it dwells softly on its inversion, the seventh that initiates the principal theme. Meanwhile, half-tone trills in the strings fade away gradually as players drop out one by one until only the last desks remain.

Royal Flush (1981) is a concerto grosso for brass quintet and orchestra commissioned by the Montreal Symphony Orchestra. The two trumpets, horn, trombone, and tuba that constitute the concertino group usually function as a unified block. They are set apart from the rest of the orchestra either by being assigned unique material or by alternating as a group with other instruments in the performance of shared material. One important consideration in the choice of *Royal Flush* for inclusion in this chapter is the incorporation of jazz elements such as blues figures and syncopated rhythms within a serious concert work. [6] (Refer to example 6-12 for an illustration of jazz traits in two of the main themes.) Freedman asserts an important distinction between *Royal Flush* and the other concerto discussed earlier in this chapter, *Celebration* of 1977. While *Celebration* owes its initial inspiration to jazz, it contains certain elements from serious art music that have been adapted for use within this orientation. *Royal Flush*, on the other hand, emanates from the domain of serious art music, but is coloured by certain elements from the world of jazz. Freedman contends that it is not simply a matter of degree, a preponderance of jazz in one and serious art music in the other. Rather, it is a matter of the intent of the composer: one is fundamentally a jazz piece, the other a serious piece of art music, with each making use of certain elements from the other's domain.

The opening gesture of *Royal Flush* consists of nine parallel lines comprising segments of octatonic scales, indicated by brackets in example 6-11. Each vertical slice of the texture contains nine different pitches separated from one another by three to six semitones. The result is a modified, less dense version of the moving cluster chords described earlier in *Nocturne III*.

An octatonic orientation is also suggested in some of the most prominent thematic material. Example 6-12 shows two important themes in superposition at Rehearsal 16, their octatonic segments indicated by brackets.

In his sketches for *Royal Flush* Freedman labels and organizes a variety of elements prior to embarking on the compositional process. The chord succession at Rehearsal 16 was planned in a particularly intriguing manner. The sketches contain a series of five-note chords, numbered consecutively from 1 to 9. Successive chords in the series evolve

Example 6-11: *Royal Flush,* measures 1 to 5, strings

Example 6-12: *Royal Flush,* Rehearsal 16+1 to 16+7, first trumpet, violins, and violas

gradually by semitonal increments, so there is a continuity in pitch content during the evolution from first to ninth chord. Freedman also dictates the order in which these closely related chords will be used: 3 7 6 5 3 5 1 3 5 3 1 2 1 3 5 3 5 3 1 2 8 9 1 2 3 5 3 6. In realizing his sketches in the score (Rehearsal 16+1 to 16+11), he uses his chords in the planned order, but he applies them to an active melodic line. Each chord retains the content and distribution of its intervals, but it is almost always transposed from its appearance in the original sketch. Thus the interval relationships within each individual chord are controlled, but those between successive chords are not. Clearly, the literal continuity of actual pitches was not a crucial factor for Freedman in this instance (examples 6-13.1 and 6-13.2).

Example 6-13.1: *Royal Flush*, sketches, page 1, staves 11 and 12

Example 6-13.2: *Royal Flush*, Rehearsal 16+1 to 16+5, brass quintet

Freedman's musical sketches for this work attest to his interest in exploring the compositional possibilities inherent in predetermined associations among various musical parameters. In one instance he focused on the relationship between melody and instrumentation. He wrote out four different melodic gestures, numbered 2, 3, 4, and 5,[7] then dictated the order in which they were to be heard (5 3 5 2 3 5 4 2 4 5 4 3 2). He then prepared a chart in which he associated each melodic gesture with a specific group of instruments. His realization of these ideas in the score (Rehearsal 17+4 to 19+5) is comparatively strict, with only one reversal in order number and minor deviations in assigned instrumentation.

Several phrases in Freedman's written notes for *Royal Flush* provide additional evidence that he was attempting to assign some of his musical parameters unique sets of collateral elements. An association between certain instruments and specific pitches is suggested by the phrase 'the tune ends with the brass and perc. reiterating the rhythm on his (their) note(s) in the motto texture.' A relationship between particular percussion instruments and specific rhythms is implied by phrases such as 'another percussion playing its rhythm,' and a further relationship between the percussion instruments that play those rhythms and certain instrumental partners is indicated by the phrase '3rd percussion and its brass partner(s) begin rhythm which evolves into another tune, which breaks off for 4th percussion and his partner.' In the score the planned associations between rhythm and instrumentation are faithfully carried out, initially. At Rehearsal 14–4, the percussion section takes centre stage for the first time. Four percussion groups (timpani, timbales on the shell, bongos and conga, and two tambourines on tom-toms) are introduced in turn, each performing an ostinato featuring its own unique rhythm. The ostinati are indicated in example 6-14, which begins with the third entry.

Example 6-14: *Royal Flush*, Rehearsal 15–4 to 15+4, percussion

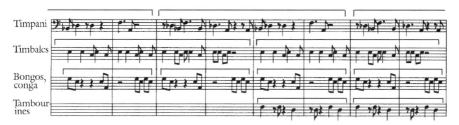

At Rehearsal 17–4, these rhythms are taken over by the strings: tambourine rhythm played by first violin, timpani by second violin, timbales by violas, and bongos by cello. Immediately thereafter, each rhythm acquires an associate in the brass quintet. From Rehearsal 17+1 to 19–3, the tambourine rhythm is played by first trumpet, the timpani rhythm by second trumpet, the timbales rhythm by horn and tuba, and bongo rhythm by the trombone. At Rehearsal 19 the percussion instruments restate their rhythmic patterns with one modification: tambourines and timbales exchange their rhythms. Following a full bar of rest, Freedman begins gradually to unravel the web of associations he has established. At Rehearsal 20 the first trumpet doubles with the tambourine, thus maintaining their association, but together they now execute the rhythm associated with the timbales. In the next entry, the bongos and conga play their assigned rhythm, but they are doubled by horn and tuba rather than by trombone. At Rehearsal 21+9, the established relationship is maintained between second trumpet and the timpani rhythm and between the horn and tuba and the timbales rhythm. However, the first trumpet and trombone exchange their rhythmic associations. After an intervening section of unrelated material the rhythmic patterns return, now completely dissociated from their original instrumentation. At Rehearsal 35, for example, the trombone doubles with the timbales rather than the bongos and conga, and together they play the timpani's rhythm rather than that previously associated with either instrumental group. Soon thereafter, strings and woodwinds join to build a complex, multilayered texture. By Rehearsal 39 ten different instruments are involved in five competing rhythmic layers: the timpani rhythmic pattern in two out-of-phase layers, the tambourine rhythmic pattern also in two out-of-phase layers, and the pattern associated with the bongos and congas in a fifth layer. Concurrently, various other instruments treat the incipit of one of the principal themes in imitative fashion. This chaotic moment apparently signals closure, since Freedman then abandons the four rhythmic patterns entirely, refocusing instead on earlier thematic material.

The *Symphony no. 3* of 1983 is a serious and substantial work, held by Freedman to be an especially important one in his output. He has always made a distinction in precompositional procedures between serious works and those in a lighter vein; serious works apparently dictate a basis of abstract or theoretical ideas to be worked out meticulously before the actual writing can begin. *Symphony no. 3* seems to have given him a greater than usual amount of difficulty in the formative stages. The sketches are covered with erasures, crossings out, and repeated modifications of his ideas, indicating that he agonized considerably over both his materials and their development. His unusually extensive search for suitable abstract ideas bears witness to his almost self-consciously systematized approach to this work. For example, in the sketches he examines a number of twelve-tone rows with their attendant possibilities for development. He also experiments with various East Indian rhythms as source material, and creates a number of numerical charts to test the relative frequency of certain compositional elements. Perhaps the most powerful theoretical influ-

ence on the symphony came from the ideas about musical space pro-
pounded by Robert Cogan in his then-recently published book, *Sonic
Design*.[8] However, Freedman makes it clear that what he read in *Sonic
Design* did not influence him in a direct way; it merely sensitized him
to the notion of space, and certain sonorities occupying certain segments of it. Given Freedman's long-held interest in the visual arts, it is
not surprising that he found inspiration in Cogan's graphs. They provided a tangible link between the visual and aural worlds, and a literal
representation of musical sound that must have had a powerful appeal
for Freedman.

Symphony no. 3 is traditional in structure, with three discrete movements, fast, slow, fast. Thematic recurrence is common, not only within
but, exceptionally for Freedman, also among movements. Indeed,
whole sections are reiterated more or less exactly, especially in the
third movement, which approximates a sonata design. A number of
motives are also carried from movement to movement. For example,
the undulations about a principal pitch seen at the opening of the first
movement reappear in modified form as undulations in the piccolo
solo that opens the second, and the use of a rhythmicized, repeated-
note motive is prominent in all three movements. Freedman's intention to integrate the movements is underscored by his use of
continuous rehearsal numbers throughout the symphony.

Despite the ubiquity of time signatures, much of the work is metrically amorphous. The pervasiveness of syncopation and irregular sub-
divisions of the beat effectively eliminate any sense of regular pulse for
long stretches of time, especially when two or more rhythmically
diverse layers are sounding together.[9] Much of the action in the first
movement is propelled by small motives, and his sketches suggest that
many of these are based on East Indian rhythms. In his plan for the section at Rehearsal 5, Freedman describes 'widely spaced tamtam, gongs,
harp (& piano?) in one of 4 rhythms (East Indian) but much slower
(augmented).' He also refers to passages of rapid repeated notes as
'compressed Hindu rhythms.'[10] These rhythms first appear briefly at
Rehearsal 3+6, then more prominently at Rehearsal 9 in the basses and
cellos. Freedman also uses the rhythms to experiment for the first time
in his career with the ancient technique of hocket. The first hint of the
technique occurs at Rehearsal 10+1 to 10+3, where repeated-note
rhythms alternate between B^{b2} in the timpani and G^4 in the viola, each
being silent while the other is playing. The hocket idea is more fully
realized at Rehearsal 16+2 to 17+7, where three different layers alter-

nate in a similar manner. However, it is not until the opening of the third movement that the idea is brought to its fullest development. At this point, the hocket begins with three different layers but quickly evolves into five, played variously by seven different instrumental groups. Each layer performs a short rhythmic burst before lapsing briefly into silence and transferring the action to another layer. Since all instruments are sounding A^{b4}, the interest is focused not only on the composite rhythm formed by the superposed layers but also on the changing colours in each layer. The effect is a strikingly new one for Freedman. A portion of the passage is shown in example 6-15.

Example 6-15: *Symphony no. 3*, Rehearsal 37–3 to 37+5

The first movement is based on the twelve-tone row shown in example 6-16.1. In the opening pages the row is deployed as four superposed trichordal segments. One pitch from each trichord is projected as the principal pitch by its long duration, the other two pitches being featured as brief undulating departures before the principal pitch reasserts itself. Four independent lines thus sound concurrently, each unique with respect to melodic figure, rhythmic pattern, timbre, and registral space, while collectively comprising the aggregate. The trichordal segmentation of the row is supplanted at Rehearsal 2 by a more complex procedure in which overlapped or nested segments of two to five pitch classes are extracted for use as independent motives, numbered in the sketches 1 through 6. Freedman's segmentation of the row is reproduced in example 6-16.1, and its realization in the score in example 6-16.2.

Example 6-16.1: *Symphony no. 3*, sketches, page 1

Example 6-16.2: *Symphony no. 3*, Rehearsal 2+3 to 2+6

By Rehearsal 4 Freedman draws some motives from inverted forms of the row, and later still begins to modify them by altering the size of some of the component intervals. Freedman clearly believes that once a motive has been established it need not retain its original intervallic relationships provided it retains its general shape or rhythm.

Unusually for Freedman in a serious work during this period, the third movement is built around a focal pitch. A^{b4} is prominent at crucial junctures throughout the movement, its predominance generally assured by heavy doubling at the unison. The passage from the opening of the movement to Rehearsal 38 provides a good example, with A^{b4} the focal pitch for ten distinct instrumental groups. Of the final ninety-six measures of the movement, fully eighty-three highlight A^{b4}, usually as the only representation of that pitch class, though on several occasions it is doubled in various octaves. In fact, Freedman uses multiple doubling to explore and define the extremes of range for pitch class A^b in this movement. From Rehearsal 62+3 to 62+12 he encompasses the lower portion of the range in a fivefold doubling of pc A^b, from A^{b1} through A^{b5}, while from Rehearsal 63 to 64 he encompasses the higher portion, also with fivefold doubling of pc A^b, from A^{b2} through A^{b6}. Significantly, he waits until the final sonority of the movement (at Rehearsal 67+14) to bracket the entire field, with sixfold doubling from A^{b1} through A^{b6}, thus neatly defining the total range for that pivotal pitch class.

These are but a few examples of Freedman's increasingly conscious use of musical space in both the vertical and horizontal dimensions, and of sonority, register, and density as definers of that space. It is not that Freedman has taken a completely new approach to musical space, although some new techniques are explored here. It is mostly that ideas that had been in rudimentary form in earlier works emerge in more evolved form, and that Freedman is now thinking consciously, even systematically, about the placement and control of musical elements in space.

The precompositional notes offer a glimpse of his heightened sensitivity to space, colour, and texture. An extract from the notes for the first movement states: 'The two lines create a recognizable pattern or texture, beginning very close and intertwining, then moving in contrary motion, then parallel, 2 8ves apart, then 3 and working back to close, intertwining texture which is suddenly interrupted by widely-spaced tam-tam/gongs, harp.' The sketches give many other hints of his interest in register and colour. The notes for the first movement speak of 'incorporating the 4 lines of the opening in their relative registers,' and the notes for the third describe 'a very lyrical contrapuntal section in which every instrument is featured as a solo instrument, sometimes briefly, sometimes longer, and always taking over from an instrument in the same range and giving way to another. The effect is one of constantly shifting colour as each line is carried by 3 or 4 different colours.'

Freedman's enhanced interest in space, colour, and texture is evident right from the beginning of the symphony. The first fifty-three measures of the first movement (to Rehearsal 5a) consist almost exclusively of long, superposed, repetitive lines, in each layer of which a sustained principal pitch is relieved periodically by a brief flourish of subsidiary pitches. As a result of this melodic homogeneity, the attention of the listener is drawn throughout this section toward registral placement, total range, textural density, and instrumental colour. The movement opens with four widely dispersed lines, each occupying its own registral space with no overlap. This texture changes abruptly at Rehearsal 2+1, which is marked by new and expanded instrumentation, by a decrease in total range and concomitant increase in density, and by registral overlap among contiguous instruments. There follows a sequence of short abutting passages unified by motivic content and number of layers (four) but strongly differentiated by dramatic changes in total range and instrumental colour. At Rehearsal 4+1 the four layers have a dark colouring, with first and second bassoon, violas, and cellos inextricably intertwined within the compressed total range of a minor ninth (C^3 to D^{b4}). Immediately following, at Rehearsal 4+7, there is a radical change both in instrumentation (oboe, horn, tuba, and basses) and in total range, which expands to a sparsely populated four octaves (D^2 to E^{b6}). Finally, at Rehearsal 5+1 the instrumental colour becomes homogeneous (first and second violins, violas, and cellos) and the motives from the previous section are displaced inward by one or more octaves, thereby compressing the total range once again to a minor ninth (D^3 to E^{b4}). This appears to be a conscious manipulation of musical space by abrupt and striking modifications in the register, range, density, and timbre of juxtaposed segments.

This block-like approach is augmented by various techniques involving a more incremental expansion and contraction of musical space. Freedman has long utilized various 'wedge' techniques to gradually alter total range and density. In order to build tension he often begins with one sustained pitch and progressively adds others that are also sustained, resulting in a cumulative increase in density. He frequently creates an oblique wedge by beginning with the lowest pitch and adding successively higher ones, or vice versa. On other occasions, he forms a more symmetrical wedge by beginning with a pitch in the middle of the range and working outwards. Normally, in order to diffuse tension he simply reverses these processes, but in the second movement of *Symphony no. 3* we encounter a new development in dissipating a dense, wide-ranged sonority. At Rehearsal 24, the method used to build the tension is familiar: divisi strings build downward from single pitch (E^6) in an oblique wedge shape. While the top pitch E^6 remains, increasingly lower pitches are added and sustained beneath it until A^{b1} is reached, ultimately creating a densely packed chord with a four-and-a-half-octave span. However, to dissipate this chord, instead of simply reversing the wedge as he often did in earlier works he gradually eliminates notes from the middle of the wedge, progressively working outwards until only the top and bottom notes remain. Finally the top note disappears and only A^b, the pivotal pitch class of the movement, remains.

Another experiment with musical space focuses on the control of linear events by means of the registral placement of pitches in vertical sonorities. The third movement features a progressive set of stretti, with rather complex derivations and interrelationships described in the notes though not fully realized in the score. Rehearsal 41 provides the first instance of stretto writing, a texture that recurs frequently in the movement. The sketches reveal that the short stretti were designed to emanate from and extend horizontally the preceding vertical sonority. First the top note of the sonority was to initiate a stretto passage, then the sonority was to recur, followed by another stretto passage initiated now by the second highest pitch of the sonority. A further repetition of the sonority was then to be followed by a stretto passage beginning on the third highest pitch, and so on. Clearly, his intention was to use the spatial arrangement of a vertical sonority to determine the order and registral placement of initial stretto notes. However, as is so often the case with Freedman, he modified his initial inspiration somewhat when it came time to realize it in practice, as an examination of the score will show. Nevertheless, the sketches confirm that spatial considerations were paramount for Freedman in planning this passage.

The final example from this symphony demonstrates Freedman's growing fascination with providing each strand in the texture with a special personality by means of colour. At Rehearsal 38 in the third movement, the unique pitch that is assigned to each of the five string parts is first rendered distinct by being supplied with its own repeated rhythmic pattern. Each string part's pitch is doubled by a changing series of wind instruments, lending further definition to that pitch. The technique thus has the effect of imbuing each pitch with a changing colour to offset the regularity of the repeated rhythmic pattern (example 6-17).

In 1984 Freedman was commissioned by the National Ballet of Canada to compose the music for the ballet *Oiseaux exotiques*. The work is an important exemplar of his ability to adapt bona fide folk idioms to his eclectic style. The exotic birds referred to in the title are not literally reflected in the music, as is the case in Messiaen's work of the same name; the birds in this work are simply represented in the costumes and scenery. The music for the ballet is based on authentic Venezuelan dance tunes that Freedman transcribed from tapes obtained from a library in Venezuela. He made a careful study of that material along with relevant historical background before undertaking the composi-

Example 6-17: *Symphony no. 3*, Rehearsal 39–3 to 39+4

tion of the work. On its completion it gained immediate popularity, in part because most listeners were already familiar with the rhythms, harmonies, tonalities, and structural models used, but also because they were intrigued by the work's exoticism and exuberance.

The suite from *Oiseaux exotiques* consists of a series of individual dances, each entirely separated from its neighbours. Along with some well-known types of dances like 'Samba' and 'Conga,' there are also a number of less familiar ones such as 'Joropo,' 'Pescadores,' and 'Llanero.' Orchestral colour plays a particularly important role in imbuing each dance with its own particular character. To achieve his purposes Freedman augments a traditional symphonic orchestra with a large battery of exotic percussion instruments such as guiro, maracas, congo drums, and cowbells. As always with Freedman, orchestral colour is an integral part of the compositional process. His sketches provide clear evidence that he does not wait until the final stages of composition before deciding on the orchestration. In fact, he maintains that he often receives his initial inspiration from colour rather than from pitch or rhythm. By this stage in his career, he felt entirely comfortable with the orchestra, and in this work he admits that he revelled in his full knowledge and control of the instruments.

Oiseaux exotiques owes much of its energy and vitality to the prevalence of rhythms that emanate directly from, or are inspired by, those found in Venezuelan dance tunes. As one might expect, syncopation is pervasive, as are changing and cross rhythms and metres. Example 6-18 demonstrates the superposition of three metrically distinct rhythmic layers. The violins and bass guitar are in 3/4 metre, the lower strings in 6/8, and the horns in 2/4. The hemiola effect in the violins in the fourth and fifth measures of the example causes a temporary coincidence with the 2/4 metre of the horn. The supporting rhythmic ostinati in the accompanying percussion instruments are omitted from the example.

Example 6-18: *Oiseaux exotiques*, 'Llanero,' page 63, Rehearsal 7+1 to 7+7

There are numerous instances of the common technique of alternating measures of 6/8 and 3/4, one famous example of which is 'Everything's Free in America,' from Leonard Bernstein's *West Side Story*. This kind of regular alternation between 6/8 and 3/4 metres is frequently supplanted in *Oiseaux exotiques* by an irregular succession of these metres, a technique commonly found in jazz. The effect apparently so intrigued Freedman that he featured it prominently in such later works as *Touchings* (1989) and *Marigold* (1996). In example 6-19, from the 'Pas de deux,' a random sequence of 3/4 and 6/8 metres in the clarinets, oboes, and first flute is accompanied by a heavily syncopated but nonetheless distinct 3/4 in the rest of the orchestra.

Example 6-19: *Oiseaux exotiques*, 'Pas de deux,' page 72, Rehearsal 4+1 to 4+9

Many of the dances are frankly tonal, indeed even supplied with key signatures. Triads and seventh chords are the most prevalent sonorities, though these chords are often coloured by the addition of other tones. In these instances, the primacy of the chordal constituents is typically clarified through such means as doubling, repetition, duration, or registral placement, while the non-chord tones are normally accorded a subordinate status. Example 6-18, shown earlier, offers a good illustration. The passage is clearly in E minor, encompassing the entirely traditional harmonic vocabulary of tonic, subdominant, and dominant, and virtually all of the non-chord tones can be construed as passing notes, appoggiaturas, and the like.

The sectional nature of the writing is evident not only on a large scale, with successive dances distinctly differentiated from one another, but at the local level as well. Each individual dance consists of discrete and readily discernible formal divisions, and most dances are unified by varied or exact recurrence of both large and small segments. Representative of these characteristics is 'Llanero' (pages 55 to 66), whose sectional structure is very traditional. A four-bar succession of chords (usually tonic-subdominant-dominant) is repeated in a chaconne-like manner, with continuous variation of the melodic line above (example 6-20).

Example 6-20: *Oiseaux exotiques*, 'Llanero,' pages 55 to 56, measures 3 to 14

Somewhat more complex is 'Joropo' (pages 19 to 30) which consists largely of a succession of eight-bar units, often in parallel periodic structure with a half close at the midpoint and a full close at the end. The eight-bar norm is occasionally curtailed by omission or elision of the final portion of the unit, as at Rehearsal 12+7. On other occasions, the eight-bar unit is extended by insertion of material before the cadence or by transforming the final measures into a transitional passage, as seen in the concluding measures of example 6-21, below. However, these modifications are insufficient to vitiate the sectional structure of the dance. Essentially, 'Joropo' is a series of variations on a pattern rather than on a theme. The characteristic eight-bar length, anacrusis, syncopes, and tonic termination of the original are retained frequently enough to serve as the model for subsequent variations. Example 6-21 provides a good illustration of the eight-measure units that form the basis of 'Joropo,' and also gives a flavour of the intricate contrapuntal interplay and colourful orchestration that are featured in virtually all of the dances in *Oiseaux exotiques*.

In 1984 Freedman's contributions to Canadian music were recognized in a tangible way with his appointment as an Officer of the Order of Canada. His prominence with the ordinary public was further enhanced through his appearance in 1986 as host of the CBC-TV series 'Music on a Sunday Afternoon.' The University of Toronto's Faculty of Music recognized Freedman's now-established reputation as a composer by inviting him to teach orchestration and composition during the years 1989–91, and by appointing him as the Jean A. Chalmers Chair Visiting Professor in the Faculty of Music for the 1990–91 academic year.

Throughout the 1980s his artistic sensibilities were being enriched and broadened on a regular basis through his association with a group of artists that called itself 'The Loons.' In addition to Freedman, the membership included musicians John Weinzweig, Harry Somers, Jack Behrens, Alex Pauk, and Alexina Louie. Writers Margaret Laurence, Sylvia Fraser, Adele Wiseman, and Helen Weinzweig formed part of the group along with poets Gwendolyn MacEwen and Miriam Waddington. The visual arts were represented in the group by painters Ron Bloore and Tony Urquhart and sculptor David Partridge. 'The Loons' met monthly to discuss recent artistic developments in the various spheres represented among them, their discussions occasionally leading to cooperative interdisciplinary performances by the 'Looner Ensemble.'

Example 6-21: *Oiseaux exotiques*, 'Joropo,' pages 24 to 26, Rehearsal 6+1 to 9–2

Throughout the mid-1980s Freedman's productivity as a composer continued unabated. However, these years were not easy ones for him on a personal level. Between 1983 and 1988 he underwent extensive psychoanalysis, a process that he found extremely painful and disturbing, though he claims that psychoanalysis ultimately proved to be both liberating and inspirational for him. While he now feels somewhat equivocal about many of the works he wrote during those turbulent years of psychoanalysis, he has been pleased with almost every work he has written since that time. He is particularly fond of the composition we shall deal with next, a landmark work in which he finally finds a satisfactory solution to the dilemma posed by the use of jazz within a serious work.

The CBC commissioned *Borealis* for the Northern Encounters Festival in 1997. The work was written for symphony orchestra and four choirs, all very appropriately represented in the festival by groups from northern countries: the Toronto Symphony, the Elmer Iseler Singers, and the Toronto Children's Choir, all from Canada, along with the Swedish Radio Choir and the Danish National Radio Choir. The concert took place in the Barbara Frum Atrium of the Canadian Broadcasting Centre, a particularly felicitous venue since it allowed the placement of the choirs around the hall to enhance antiphonal effects. Following its performance, *Borealis* received high acclaim from the UNESCO-sponsored International Rostrum of Composers in Paris. During this event, broadcasters from all over the world presented works they had aired on radio during the past year. Of the sixty works presented from thirty-two countries, *Borealis* was ranked fourth.

The choral text for most of the piece has no intrinsic meaning, consisting of words Freedman created himself simply because he liked their sound. The single exception occurs at the climactic moment of the piece (Rehearsal 28), which is heralded by a dramatic sentence in English: 'And yet there is only one great thing, the only thing, to live to see in huts & on journeys the great day that dawns, and the light that fills the world.' This is an excerpt from *Anerca*, a collection of poems made by explorer Knud Rasmussen and translated by Edmund Carpenter. Because the choirs have used only meaningless sounds to this point in the piece, the appearance of comprehensible text close to the end of the work is especially striking.

Freedman believes *Borealis* to be a summation of much that had gone before in his stylistic development. In particular, the work is an important representation of the new, more North American style in which his harmonic language makes extensive use of scales derived from a typical jazz chord. *Borealis* also marks the crest of a long line of experiments with texture. We shall examine a representative selection of textures in *Borealis*, as well as various manifestations of Freedman's special scales.

Although *Borealis* is strongly flavoured both harmonically and thematically with Freedman's jazz-based scales, the work is absolutely devoid of any jazz elements, either in sound or in concept. Freedman traces the source of these scales to a favourite jazz chord, the dominant seventh with flattened fifth, added blues third, and thirteenth. Freedman explains that in order to use these components in the form of a scale he had to fill in some of the gaps in that chord. He began by adding a major ninth above the thirteenth. Assuming C as root, the resultant chord became C E G^b B^b E^b A D. He then added an augmented eleventh above the major ninth, yielding the chord C E G^b B^b E^b A D F$^\#$. The elimination of the obvious duplication between the flattened fifth and the augmented eleventh produced the chord C E B^b E^b A D F$^\#$ and the seven-note scale C D E^b E F$^\#$ A B^b, one of Freedman's two jazz-based scales. His second scale was formed by the addition of an unflattened fifth to produce, in his words, 'a wonderfully rich sonority which translated into an equally effective scale.' The insertion of pc G resulted in the chord C E G B^b E^b A D F$^\#$ and the eight-note scale, C D E^b E F$^\#$ G A B^b. Although the added note (in this case G) is often used in an auxiliary or supplemental capacity, Freedman uses his eight-note scale nearly as commonly as his seven-note one. The pc set classes to which these scales belong, along with their interval class successions, are summarized as follows:

7-28:	0		1		3		5		6		7		9	
ics:		1		2		2		1		1		2		(3)
8-27:	0		1		2		4		5		7		8		10
ics:		1		1		2		1		2		1		2		(2)

Given that C is the nominal root of the chords that generate his scales (in the iterations spelled out above), it is interesting that Freedman finds both scales most congenial in sound when they are arranged beginning on B^b (interval class succession 2 2 1 1 2 3 for his seven-note scale and 2 2 1 1 2 1 2 for his eight-note scale). However, he cautions that the initial pitch class when the scales are so ordered is not to be construed as a tonic in any sense.[11]

In numerous places in the score, pc set classes 7-28 and 8-27 can be interpreted as possible sources of individual melodic gestures or in isolated simultaneities. For example, every melodic or harmonic event on the first page of the score except for the chromatic line of the vibraphone can be referred to pc set 7-28 or 8-27, often as a subset. However, each harmonic or melodic event uses a different set of pitch classes, and the scale patterns are frequently inversions of Freedman's normal arrangements. Given the very clear manifestations of his scales at other places in the score, it seems likely that such apparent uses as appear on the first page are purely coincidental and have no significance. Freedman confirms that he did not consciously combine different pitch iterations of his scales, use the inverted form of either scale, or make use of subsets. He says that any of these may have occurred fortuitously, but he affirms that he did none of them deliberately. On the other hand, his scales may initially have been used more frequently than is apparently the case. Given his antipathy toward rigidity and his willingness to modify a preconceived design or procedure to obtain a better sound, one can't be certain that he did not intentionally employ one of his scales, only to alter one or more pitches subsequently to suit the needs of the moment.

However, there are many places in the score where the use of the scales is unequivocal rather than conjectural. The first such place is at Rehearsal 13–1, where the top line of the texture projects pc set class 8-27 as a simple scale in ungapped ascending form (example 6-22).

Example 6-22: *Borealis*, Rehearsal 13–1 to 13+1, flutes, oboes, and clarinets

Strictly stepwise projections of these scales are unusual in Freedman's usage, and may well have been a deliberate attempt to sensitize the listener to this new harmonic language that was to form such an important part of the subsequent action. Other unequivocal appearances of the scales can be found from Rehearsal 20 to Rehearsal 21, Rehearsal 22 to Rehearsal 23, Rehearsal 27+6 to Rehearsal 28, and Rehearsal 31+1 to Rehearsal 31+4.

In *Borealis* Freedman focuses more intensely than ever before upon the domain of texture. Broad, dense textures reminiscent of those of Ligeti or Penderecki are no longer sporadic occurrences; they occupy a large proportion of the work, usually in close juxtaposition with one another. Each has a distinct character and stands in stark contrast with neighbouring textures. For the most part Freedman favours homogeneous instrumentation within a given texture, with a particular interest in sound masses consisting of densely packed divisi strings. Never amorphous, his textures generally embody an ongoing and clearly perceptible internal process.

The work begins quietly and mysteriously with a soft, sustained chord by six solo strings in harmonics, followed immediately by a sustained C^4 in horn, marimba, and harp. The opening chord is echoed by a similar chord in the woodwinds, punctuated by nervous gestures in thirty-second notes by the harp and marimba. Meanwhile, the sustained C^4 is gradually augmented by D^{b4} and D^4 to form a tight cluster, a process that is reversed at the end of the work. The stage has been set for the upper line of the strings to introduce and develop a haunting motive consisting of a sustained note followed in succession by a falling minor second, rising major seventh, and falling major third, as shown in example 6-23. This line also initiates a leisurely unfolding of the twelve-tone row (P0 = 1 0 11 7 3 10 4 9 8 6 5 2) which, along with Freedman's jazz-based scales, governs much of the pitch organization in *Borealis*.

Example 6-23: *Borealis*, Rehearsal 1+1 to 1+5

Example 6-23 also demonstrates a texture that probably evolved from Freedman's 'thickened melody' technique in which the melodic line is supported from below by tightly clustered lines, each of which replicates the melodic contour beginning at a different pitch level. At

Rehearsal 1 the melodic line is accompanied in a similar manner by closely packed divisi strings. However, although all parts generally follow the contour of the melodic line, they do not always replicate its intervallic structure. Freedman achieves dramatic effect by increasing the total range of the texture when there are large upward leaps in the melodic line. His thickened melody has now been enhanced with carefully planned variations in amplitude.

At Rehearsal 3 the opening motive is given a new colour when the four choirs enter in turn to intone it softly on the syllable 'oo.' A dramatic tempo change at Rehearsal 6 heralds the arrival of a new, purely instrumental section characterized by progressive accretion and reduction in a succession of juxtaposed sound masses. Beginning at Rehearsal 6+3 there is a thirty-four-measure divisi string passage featuring several different methods of handling a homogeneous sound mass. At the outset, each string section is divided into eight parts that function as a unit. The passage begins with an overlapping succession of quasi-cumulative expansions. There are eight such expansions (two for each string section), each of which begins at the unison and works away from that point, growing eventually to an eight-part sustained sonority. Just as each individual expansion builds outward from a single pitch, the composite of such expansions builds outward from a single group, eventually resulting in densely packed thirty-two-part simultaneities. The third, fourth, and fifth expansions are shown in example 6-24.

At Rehearsal 9 the strings coalesce into a brief sixteen-part homorhythmic passage that terminates with a staggered reduction from sixteen parts to one, each part ending on B^3. The uppermost of the first violin parts is the last to complete the passage, descending two and a half octaves from $F^{\#6}$ to B^3 via a fourteen-note sequence of pitches in steady eighth notes. Each of the other parts had ended earlier with a segment of different size from the end of the same fourteen-note pitch succession for its own measured descent to the final B^3. Each of the sixteen parts uses a different duration as the basis for its descent, allowing the passage to drift raggedly to a conclusion, as seen in example 6-25.

The section that follows is dominated by choral humming and chanting. Taking its departure from the terminal pitch of the previous section (B^3), the choral sound grows incrementally from a single part to a dense simultaneity of twenty-two unique pitches encompassing the aggregate. At Rehearsal 13 the choirs suddenly change to a

Example 6-24: *Borealis*, Rehearsal 7+3 to 7+8

homorhythmic texture, using words such as 'shaba,' 'tagachio,' and 'chagatu' to introduce a new motive, as seen in example 6-26.

The focus shifts at Rehearsal 15+7 from a massed, unified choral texture to a purely instrumental, multilayered texture. Dense and intricately contrapuntal, this section stands in stark contrast with the

Example 6-25: *Borealis*, Rehearsal 9+4 to 9+10, divisi strings

homogeneous sound mass that immediately precedes it. There are five discrete layers in the texture. Common to all layers is the pitch content, a single representation of pc set class 8-27 (Freedman's eight-tone jazz-based scale). These pitch classes are deployed in short segments, articulated by rests or sustained notes. The first layer consists of high woodwinds, xylophone, and vibraphone performing sixteenth-note

Example 6-26: *Borealis*, Rehearsal 15–4 to 15–1

groups. Although the five parts rise and fall synchronously, each is assigned a different segment of the scale. The instruments in both the second and third layers (first and second violins, viola, and marimba in one group, and trumpets and horns in the other) utilize material, similar to that of the first layer, but differ slightly in the temporal space occupied, so that the highest pitches in each layer occur at different times. The fourth and fifth layers differ markedly, both from one another and from the first, second, and third layers. The fourth layer (unison trombones) features sustained pitches and falling glissandi while the fifth (bass clarinet and cellos) concentrates on triplet figures. At the conclusion of the section, shown in example 6-27, the underlying scale is featured in strict stepwise descent in all parts, which eventually converge on C^4.

Rehearsal 17 reverts to the opening tempo and material, and thenceforth the elements already presented are developed and expanded. The final portion of the piece is particularly interesting in that Freedman explicitly demonstrates the relationship between his two scales (pc set classes 7-28 and 8-27) and distinguishes both from their broader chromatic backdrop. At Rehearsal 31+1 seven wind instruments each play two pitches in alternation, the hegemony of one over the other ensured by longer duration of the principal pitch. Collectively those seven principal tones (pcs 2, 3, 5, 7, 8, 9, and 11) comprise a version of pc set class 7-28, while the addition of the auxiliary pitches completes the aggregate. This complex is preceded, accompanied, and followed by aleatoric gestures in a number of instruments on pitch classes 0, 2, and 3. The addition of new pc 0 to the principal tones of the woodwinds yields a version of pc set class 8-27 (pcs 0, 2, 3, 5, 7, 8, 9, and 11), the literal superset of pc set class 7-28. This short passage neatly illustrates the relationship between Freedman's seven-tone and eight-tone scales, and the supplementary nature of the seventh element in the latter scale (example 6-28).[12]

The work ends much as it began, with a soft sustained chord by six solo strings in harmonics. This time the tight cluster of sustained pitches is gradually eroded until only the C^4 remains. The nervous instrumental gestures in thirty-second notes that appeared in the opening of the work are replaced at its end by eerie solo vocal gestures offstage, for which Freedman's eight-tone scale once again provides the tonal resources.

Borealis marks an appropriate place to complete our examination of Freedman's stylistic evolution. Freedman himself acknowledges the

Example 6-27: *Borealis*, Rehearsal 16–2 to 16+2

Example 6-28: *Borealis*, Rehearsal 31–3 to 31+4

momentous importance of this work in his output, particularly in the domains of pitch and texture. Since its composition in 1997 his productivity has continued unabated, with an average of two or three new major compositions each year.

Chapter Seven
Conclusion

The foregoing chapters have focused primarily on Freedman's stylistic evolution, from the conservative neoclassic orientation of his early works to the astonishing eclecticism of his mature output. This final chapter will focus on four important aspects of Freedman's work: the fundamental characteristics that endure in his music despite changes in style, the unique methods that he has evolved to compose his works, the interests and attitudes that have profoundly influenced his style, and the position he occupies in the context of the contemporary music scene in Canada.

Despite the many transformations that have occurred in Freedman's style over the years, a number of fundamental and enduring character-istics can be discerned. Structurally, his works have always consisted of a succession of discrete and clearly differentiated sections, carefully planned in advance with respect to both content and ordering. He seldom bases his structures on stereotypical formal models, not-withstanding the frequent appearance in his sketches of terms like 'introduction,' 'bridge,' and 'coda.' Freedman maintains that form should be moulded by content rather than by pre-existing archetypes. While recurrence is an important means of achieving unity and coher-ence in his works, the reprised material rarely appears without modifi-cation. Our recognition of it often depends more on our identification of elements such as contour, texture, or rhythm than on literal recur-rence of pitch.

Freedman's writing is rarely tonal, in the functional sense. Individ-ual sonorities range from thin, tertian-based chords, often coloured with accessory tones, to dense, massive, vertical assemblages. Triadic structures often exhibit some prominent features of jazz sonorities including both major and minor forms of the third, each sounding in a different octave, as well as flattened fifths, and major and minor ninths. At the other end of the size spectrum, Freedman sometimes stacks large numbers of tones to form skyscraper chords. These are not simply random compilations of pitches or the fortuitous results of coincident lines. The sketches bear eloquent testimony to the care he devotes to the content and distribution of their constituent pitches. Freedman attests that a primary concern in building chords is that the aggregate be encompassed within as short a space of time as possible. Often, when searching for a chordal pitch, he looks back at preceding material to see what is needed to complete the total chromatic.

Freedman has a well-developed lyrical sense, manifest in his preference for melodic lines that are not excessively disjunct. Most of his melodies are eminently singable, and many incorporate inflections that are similar to 'blue notes.' His predilection for motives based on both the prime and inverted forms of pc set class 3-5 has been evident since his very first composition. It is probably not coincidental that five different representations of this set class can be found within Freedman's favourite jazz chord. As we have seen, this chord also forms the basis of his seven-note scale (a representation of pc set class 7-28) that became such an important resource in later works. Example 7-1 begins with a rendering of that jazz chord built on C followed by the representations of pc set class 3-5 that reside within it. The example concludes with the unrhythmicized components of two jazz-based motives, also favourites of Freedman's, that can be extracted from that chord.

Example 7-1: Jazz chord based on C, and excerpts

Another motive commonly found throughout Freedman's oeuvre is a twisting figure consisting of five or more tones that reduce to a chromatic or near-chromatic collection. Freedman asserts that he derives his twisting figure from the visual arts rather than from jazz. The angularity of certain visual images evidently evokes for him a similar contour in musical tones.

Melodically, as harmonically, Freedman attempts to encompass the total chromatic within a short space of time. He believes that initially he espoused this principle as a means of avoiding tonal reminiscences, but the attractiveness of the melodic contours obtained in this way has made the practice an integral part of his technique.

Freedman's fascination with the unexpected is particularly evident in the domain of rhythm. He actively pursues this goal by means of such devices as syncopation, changing and cross metres, irregular placement of pitches within the prevailing metre, and the occasional suspension of metre or pulse. Ostinati have been an integral part of his technique since his earliest works. Frequently, the melodic components of ostinati are asynchronous with the prevailing metre, a complexity that is compounded when several ostinati are played concurrently. When the composer wishes to create a new and interesting rhythm or develop an existing one in an unusual way, he frequently has recourse to a technique he learned very early in his career from Messiaen. He creates two logical number series and interweaves them to form a new, more irregular one. For example, the interweaving of the series 2 4 6 8 (successive numbers increased by 2) and 9 6 4 3 (successive numbers decreased by 3, 2, then 1) yields the series 9 2 6 4 4 6 3 8. The application to rhythm of a series derived in this manner yields syncopations that Freedman finds fascinating.

The conscious control of texture and timbre has always been an important aspect of Freedman's craft. His works are usually organized as a succession of discrete sections that differ markedly from one another. Some sections are homogeneous with respect to content and orchestral colour, and their interest lies primarily in a single underlying developmental process. Others consist of a number of layers differentiated as to content and orchestral colour, and their focus is on contrapuntal interplay. In either case, successive sections are normally articulated by dramatic changes, often in a number of domains simultaneously. One element that almost invariably changes at a point of articulation is timbre. Freedman's years as an orchestral player have imbued him with a keen awareness of instrumental colour, and the process of orchestration is an integral part of his compositional process. When the need arises, he demands unusual sounds from both instrumentalists and vocalists. Indeed, texts for the vocal works are sometimes created by the composer himself out of words that have no inherent meaning, but possess sound qualities he finds appropriate for his purposes.

Two conflicting perspectives are in obvious competition in Freedman's compositional methods. On one hand, he actively seeks logical processes to organize his ideas and their development. The sketches confirm that he devotes much of his energy in the formative phases of a composition to evolving and testing various rational processes. On the other hand, he takes great delight in thwarting those processes once they have been established. The scores provide abundant evidence of apparently impulsive departures from ongoing logical processes. Freedman often mediates between the two perspectives by setting up *a priori* a logical process which in itself yields an irregular, unexpected result.[1] He obtains great intellectual satisfaction from knowing that something that sounds unpredictable can be explained as an outgrowth of a very logical process.

In defiance of the time-honoured belief that the shape and evolution of musical ideas are products of some indefinable, mysterious, and purely intuitive process, many composers freely acknowledge that they rely on some surprisingly methodical procedures to spawn and nurture their musical inspirations. This is certainly true of Freedman, who, quite early in his career, developed a method of composing that has clearly proved to be effective, since he claims never to have suffered from the musical equivalent of 'writer's block.' An understanding of the means he employs to conceive, mould, and develop his musical ideas is important, because these generative procedures and their underlying philosophy have a profound impact on the end product, the musical score.

In order to fulfil the obligations imposed by an average of three major commissions per year, Freedman has, of necessity, evolved an efficient and reliable approach to the task of composition. His first order of business is to study any background material that might be relevant, including works written by other composers. Following this preliminary stage he embarks on the most critical phase of the creative process. During this period, which may last as long as a week, he does not tolerate interruptions. He describes this as the time when the real work of composition is done, dismissing as 'just craft' the subsequent work of actually putting notes on the page. He begins with a careful assessment of the timbral characteristics and technical capabilities of the instruments for which the work is intended. Then he sets out quite deliberately to generate musical ideas. To many composers, musical ideas arrive first in the form of ordered pitches. This is never true with Freedman, whose ideas initially take the form of particular moods, textures, timbres, or movements. It is his standard practice to concentrate intensely, usually late at night, on the effect he is trying to create. His imagination then takes over while he sleeps. Invariably this process results in an embryonic musical idea, albeit one which has yet to be clothed with precise pitches and rhythms. Having conceived his initial idea, he finds that it quickly generates another, which in turn triggers a third, until soon he has a sizeable collection. As a musician steeped in jazz, he finds that hundreds of ideas emerge effortlessly and naturally spawn others, much as they do in jazz improvisation. 'For me,' says Freedman, 'ideas are no great problem; the problem is in choosing among them.' His next task is to sort through them, refining their content, determining what relationships exist among them, deciding whether one could lead naturally to another, rejecting those that seem impractical, and so on. A main criterion for keeping an idea is its potential for development or interaction, although occasionally he retains one entirely for its shock value, in the full knowledge that it does not harmonize well with the others.

In the next stage of his creative process, he plans the overall structure of the work, first plotting its broadest outlines, and then fleshing it out with details. Decisions are made regarding structural matters such as proportion, articulation, climax, and recurrence. Probably as an outgrowth of his work with film, Freedman is highly sensitive to the timing, length, and proportion of events in his compositions. His sketches abound with intricate calculations to determine the number of minutes and seconds a given event should occupy. He also credits his extensive film-writing experience for forcing him to be disciplined and to work quickly and confidently.

The actual step-by-step planning for a new composition takes place in a hand-written set of 'program notes.' These notes serve several purposes: they provide a logical framework within which the piece can develop, and they provide a means of keeping track of his ideas in some detail, so that he won't forget them. Sometimes the finished score conforms fairly accurately to his notes, though more often it is merely a rough approximation, having been refined or even modified dramatically as the composing process reveals problems or suggests better ideas. The prose he uses in his program notes is often colourful, betraying his long-standing interests in painting and theatre. In fact, the musical ideas themselves often originate in visual imagery or dramatic gesture. For example, in *Sonata for Symphonic Winds* (1988), he calls for a 'sweep of foliage ending on high A' and a '[t]ympany [which] interrupts with 3 or 4 impatient strokes.' In *Bones*, a marimba solo composed in 1989, the sketches call for arpeggios which 'explode.'

Example 7-2 is a reproduction of an excerpt from Freedman's handwritten notes for the first movement of his *Symphony no. 3*. The circled numbers in the left side of the page refer to the four different types of material being used in the nine successive sections covered by these notes. Also on the left side of the page are specific durations for each section. The reference to Josquin's 'Benedictus' (six lines from the bottom) suggests that Freedman saw that work as a model for the material he identifies as number 3.

Example 7-2: Notes for *Symphony no. 3*, excerpt from page 1

At some point during this intermediate stage of composition, Freedman's ideas take on definite notational shape. On a separate piece of manuscript paper he works methodically to render his ideas in more definitive form, and to work out their inherent possibilities. These sketches reveal many of the secrets of Freedman's craft, and provide fascinating glimpses into the workings of his mind. They show how his ideas are generated as well as the methods he uses to manipulate and develop them. It is often as interesting to see what he has rejected as it is to see what he has retained. Unfortunately, he does not use proper sketchbooks for this work. Instead, in his feverish haste to get his ideas down on paper he writes on anything handy, including old envelopes, hotel stationery, and unused pages from other scores. The result is often a nightmare for the researcher – a chaotic and refractory collection of loose scraps of paper. An excerpt from Freedman's sketches for the first movement of his *Symphony no. 3* is reproduced in example 7-3.

Example 7-3: Sketches for *Symphony no. 3*, excerpt from page 1

Only after a work has been carefully sketched out, as described above, is Freedman ready to begin the final stage – the writing of the actual score. In his working sketches he never casts his ideas so definitively that there is no scope for improvisation as he does the actual writing. Occasionally, his ideas change so drastically during the writing process that he is forced to tear up what he has done (an act which he describes as 'extremely painful') and begin again. Unlike many composers, Freedman does not produce a preliminary keyboard version of his work. Indeed, it would be most surprising if he were to do so, since, as he freely admits, his keyboard skills are minimal. Rather, he works in full score, quite slowly, and with very few revisions; his first draft is usually his last. He normally writes from the beginning to the end of a piece, chronologically, and he usually works on only one piece at a time. Freedman sums up his attitude toward composing this way: 'The real fun of composing is in the initial stages. The actual writing is an easy, almost inevitable process.'

By the 1960s, Freedman could predict with some degree of confidence how a work would sound before he actually heard it performed. Because he was always impatient with any effect that was too predictable, he soon began deliberately to take chances and test novel ideas whose effect he could not foresee. The first performance was thus an important learning experience that frequently prompted him to make changes in the score. While revisions made during the actual composition of a work are normally restricted to minor details, those that occur after the first performance are likely to be more substantial.

Intellectual puzzles and games have long been one of Freedman's hobbies, and his compositional sketches are liberally sprinkled with evidence of this fascination. Occasionally we see indications of what can only be described as 'doodling.' For example, on one page from his sketches he attempts to rearrange the letters of Johann Sebastian Bach's name to form another meaningful phrase, and comes up (inaccurately, as it happens) with 'John's Cabanna Tea Bins.' However, most of his self-imposed intellectual puzzles have serious compositional intent. Number series of various kinds are of particular interest, and he has found them useful in generating and manipulating material in virtually every musical domain. On one occasion he made a serious but abortive attempt to correlate the values of the Fibonacci series with various musical elements. More often, however, he creates these number series himself, frequently using techniques he learned from Messiaen. As example 7-3 reveals, cryptic sets of numbers and other markings adorn many of the pages of the sketches, posing a considerable challenge for the analyst, since Freedman himself often cannot remember their original purpose. Fortunately, it has proved possible in the majority of cases to decipher their meaning. They have been used by Freedman to control such diverse aspects of a composition as the number of voices, their order of entry, the durational distance between successive entries, the elements of a tone row with which successive entries begin, the rotation of elements in a succession of chords, and the duration of successive pitches in a pattern.

Very rarely are the subtle intricacies of Freedman's compositional processes perceptible in performance, even to a musically sophisticated listener. Though Freedman denies that their use is prompted by a desire to set up self-imposed limitations or goals, he does admit to a certain element of intellectual conceit. He is not satisfied to rely purely on instinct to guide his musical decisions, preferring to work out something intellectually that fulfils the same function. He believes that most good works of art have a logic that operates, often imperceptibly, beneath the surface. However, he does not believe that the legitimacy of a logical procedure is compromised if some element of it is altered. Indeed, as we have seen, he very frequently and deliberately undermines an ongoing rigorous process.

Thus far in this chapter I have summarized some of the enduring characteristics of Freedman's musical style as well as the methods he uses in the process of composition. My final comments will focus in a more general way on Freedman's persona as manifest in the interests and attitudes that have profoundly influenced his style, and on the position he occupies on the Canadian music scene.

In an interview early in his career with Helmut Blume,[2] Freedman was quoted as saying, 'It was these early interests – jazz and painting – that I still recognize as the predominant influences in my attitude to music,' a statement that still holds true today. It would be difficult to overstate the importance of jazz in Freedman's musical development and thought. In a literal sense, jazz-related elements such as syncopation and 'blues' inflections appear with great frequency in his work, but in a broader sense jazz influences can be inferred as well. His penchant for unpredictability and asymmetry, his facility in generating multiple variants of a single idea, and his fascination with the interface between controlled and improvised elements must surely be inspired by his lifelong infatuation with the idiom. Freedman also acknowledges the impact of the visual arts on his work. Not only does he frequently transfer visual images into musical notes, but he also draws in a more general way upon painting for inspiration. Among compositions thus inspired are *Tableau* (1952), *Images* (1958), *Pyramid of Roses* (music for a film by Chris Chapman on 'Vale Variations' by painter Harold Town, 1980), and *Graphic VI: Town* (impressions of four paintings by Harold Town, 1986).

The indigenous music of different cultures has been featured in many of Freedman's works, either in literal or stylized form. He has produced a number of arrangements of traditional Canadian folk songs, notably his *Laurentian Moods*, a setting of French-Canadian folk songs for band, 1957, and *Blue ... Green ... White ...;* an arrangement of songs of the eastern provinces for choir, 1978. Since his contact in early childhood with the Indians who came to trade at his father's store in Medicine Hat, Freedman has been keenly interested in the music and culture of Canada's native peoples, a fascination that has surfaced in a number of tangible ways. For example, he incorporated several authentic Indian melodies in *Klee Wyck*, of 1970, and used a text made up of Ontario place names taken from the Ojibwa language in *Keewaydin*, of 1971. His interest in indigenous music extends beyond the borders of Canada. The music of *Oiseaux exotiques* (1984) is based on melodic, harmonic, and rhythmic characteristics found in Venezuelan folk idioms.

Freedman has also devoted a significant amount of energy in creating works for young people. He feels passionately that if the youth of today are to become the intelligent and receptive audience of tomorrow they must be acclimated at an early stage to the contemporary musical soundscape. He has attempted to address this need through such works as *Little Acorns*, a set of graded short pieces for school band begun in 1970, *Keewaydin*, a work designed to accustom young singers to dissonant sounds, and *Tangents*, a virtual *tour de force* of contemporary techniques for accomplished young orchestral players.

Affable, approachable, and eminently likeable, Freedman is the antithesis of the image many people have of the contemporary composer as a stodgy and isolated figure. Freedman is well attuned to the demands of the real world, as evidenced not only by his stylistic eclecticism but by his pragmatic approach to modifying his scores, should the need arise.[3] Naturally gregarious, Freedman is endowed with a rich sense of humour that bubbles easily to the surface during conversation. However, he is exceedingly serious about his craft, and works painstakingly until he achieves a result that meets his exacting standards.

Freedman himself concedes that he has never been a radical figure on the Canadian musical stage. It is true that there is little in his music that could be described as unique or groundbreaking. He is not technique-driven, and hence is not interested in being at the forefront of new musical developments. While some of his more radical contemporaries focus on new sounds, techniques, and organizational procedures considered for their own sakes rather than as raw material for development, Freedman focuses on the possibilities for integrating these new phenomena into a broader musical landscape. He makes a deliberate point of experimenting with newly emerged techniques as an expedient and productive way to discover how or whether they might be incorporated into his own music. As we have seen, this practice has resulted in an extraordinarily eclectic oeuvre. He views the new ideas which emerge at the frontiers of musical development in much the same way as he views the established ideas he finds in studying the scores of older composers: all are fodder for his musical imagination, to be examined for their relevance to his particular musical purposes. Ever the pragmatist, Freedman has always, in the final analysis, been more interested in product than in process. At heart, his approach to his craft is non-cerebral. He contends that music that has to be explained before it can be understood is not worth listening to.

He attributes his unusual approach to composition in part to the fact that he was not university trained, as were most of his fellow composers. He contends that he learned his craft the way Mozart, Beethoven, and Bach did, in a one-on-one master-apprentice relationship. This is a situation that is difficult to replicate at a university. In Freedman's view, there is so much ancillary material in the core curriculum at most university music schools that there is a real risk a budding composer might lose focus. This is not likely to happen in a one-on-one learning situation, where a young composer studies only what he needs to learn in order to express himself. Freedman also stresses the importance of not only analysing but also performing the music of other composers. As a professional orchestral musician for twenty-five years, he has played an enormous amount and variety of music, and in this, too, he differs from many of his fellow composers.

Freedman describes his own music as essentially 'North American,' a style which owes much to his early roots in popular music and jazz. Because of the direct connection that popular music has with the audience, Freedman contends that he has never had to make a conscious effort to make his music accessible. He achieves this end quite naturally. As well, the jazz elements that pervade many of his works resonate easily and intelligibly in the ears of modern listeners.

Freedman will be remembered as a skilled musical craftsman with a remarkable ability to blend and adapt existing ideas into interesting new amalgams. He is comfortable in his craft, and feels neither the desire nor the compulsion to push the musical envelope as a pioneer. In an interview with Freedman shortly after his eighty-first birthday, I asked him how he thought he was perceived as a composer by his colleagues. He responded that they probably view him as neither radical nor middle-of-the-road, but rather as a maverick who goes his own way and is not interested in all the latest fashions. He added that he hoped to be remembered by future generations in just that way, 'as a maverick, a person who went his own way and tried out whatever he wanted to do, not what somebody else wanted him to do.'[4]

Whether or not he is remembered as a maverick, Freedman's real legacy is the interesting, beautifully crafted, and eclectic body of works he leaves for future generations. In writing this book I have been able to investigate many of these works, but have regrettably had to exclude a legion of others that are equally deserving of detailed study. Remarkable riches are to be found throughout Freedman's extensive oeuvre. It is my fervent hope that I have tantalized my readers sufficiently that they will be inspired to discover them for themselves.

Notes

1. Introduction

1 Beckwith 1969, 4.

2 Proctor 1980, ix.

3 *Encyclopedia of Music in Canada*, 2nd ed., ed. Helmut Kallmann, Gilles Potvin, and Kenneth Winters (Toronto: University of Toronto Press, 1992).

4 Canadian composers who have been the subjects of published monographs to date include Jean Papineau-Couture, S.C. Eckhardt-Gramatté, Serge Garant, Hugh Le Caine, Sir Ernest MacMillan, Barbara Pentland, R. Murray Schafer, Harry Somers, John Weinzweig, and Healey Willan.

5 Boothroyd 1979, Hepner 1971, Nichols 1981, Dixon 1980, Dixon 1981, Dixon 1982, and Dixon 1983.

6 These tables can be found in Allen Forte's *The Structure of Atonal Music* (New Haven: Yale University Press, 1973), 179–81, and in numerous other twentieth-century sources such as Joseph N. Straus's *Introduction to Post-tonal Theory* (New Jersey: Prentice Hall, 1990), 180–3, and John Rahn's *Basic Atonal Theory* (New York: Longman, 1980), 140–3.

7 Nevertheless, the reader is encouraged to supplement the illustrative examples by referring where possible to the full musical score of the work under discussion. The Canadian Music Centre is an excellent resource, both for scores and recordings of Freedman's works.

2. The Early Years (to 1952)

1 As a young boy in Medicine Hat Freedman recalls vividly meeting many Indians who came to his father's store to sell their fur. Freedman has never forgotten these early encounters, speculating that the Indians he met at that

time may well have been the sons of famous chiefs who had achieved their renown in historic battles. As an adult his ongoing fascination with the history of Canada's native peoples has manifested itself in a number of important musical works.

2 During his five years at the school he absorbed an aesthetic that was later to assume great importance in his musical career – the art of economy of means. He was captivated by the stunning effects which could be achieved in Japanese paintings by a very few skilful brush strokes.

3 Blume and Potvin 1964, 42.

4 The oboe countermelody of the second phrase (beginning at measure 5) also opens with a version of pc set class 3-5, now inverted from its earlier shape in measures 1 to 2 and given a new rhythmic setting.

5 Keillor 1994, 47.

6 See, for example, the second movement, Rehearsal A+8 to A+10, lower strings.

7 In the example the English horn sounds a perfect fifth lower than written. In these early works Freedman does not transpose his instruments to produce scores in C.

8 Blume and Potvin 1964, 43.

9 The first theme consists of the opening nine notes of the movement, the second theme begins at Rehearsal A–8, while the third theme begins at Rehearsal C.

10 The reader is reminded that Freedman has not yet adopted the practice of producing his scores in C at this point, so the English horn sounds a perfect fifth lower than written.

11 'Harlem Hoedown' was actually written outside the chronological framework of this chapter, but since it is an integral part of the *Matinée Suite* it will be dealt with here.

12 I have omitted the strings and brass from the example, since they simply reinforce the piano part.

13 It could be argued that it is the prime form of the row that is being projected by the theme at Rehearsal A+3, the retrograde form having been used in introductory material. No sketches exist to clarify this point, which is, in any case, of virtually no importance.

14 See, for example, the reversal of order numbers 11 and 12 of RI0 in the cello part at Rehearsal B+1.

15 Toronto: Ricordi, 1960.

16 The motto chord appears in the following locations: Rehearsals D+1 to D+3, E+1 to E+3, F+1 to F+2, G–3 to G+1, and M+1 to M+4.

3. Reaction: The Search for a Personal Language (1953 to 1961)

1 Notably, the *Suite for Piano* and the first and second movements of the
   Matinée Suite.

2 See, for example, Krenek's *Studies in Counterpoint* (New York: Schirmer,
   1940), or his article 'New Developments of the Twelve-Tone Technique,'
   Music Review 4 (1943): 81–97.

3 Furthermore, Freedman had simultaneously received an offer from Lou
   Applebaum to play in the pit orchestra at the very first Shakespearean festival in Stratford, Ontario. The opportunity to be paid to work with actors
   such as Tyrone Guthrie, Alec Guinness, and Irene Worth was too attractive
   to turn down.

4 Mary Morrison, along with soprano Phyllis Mailing, built their reputations
   in the 1960s and 1970s as specialists in the interpretation of Canadian
   works, many of which were written especially for them.

5 As we have noted earlier, pc set class 3-5 is a favourite intervallic collection
   of Freedman's.

6 The soundtrack Freedman wrote for this film features jazz, an idiom that he
   was still reluctant to allow into his serious compositions.

7 In the Berandol publication, Nakamura's first name is misspelled as
   'Kuzuo.' According to George Proctor, only the first of these three paintings
   can be traced, and was actually given a different name by Freedman. Proctor suggests that 'Blue Mountain' is in fact based on Lawren Harris's
   1927–8 painting entitled *Lake and Mountains*, now hanging in the Art
   Gallery of Ontario. (Proctor 1980, 68).

8 Proctor 1980, 68.

9 However, Freedman states that at the time he composed *Images*, he had
   never heard *Also Sprach Zarathustra*.

10 When consulting example 3-6, note that Freedman's score is not in C.

11 The missing combinations are C, C$^\#$, F$^\#$ and F$^\#$, G, C.

12 Hepner 1975, 72. Freedman states that the 'pale criss-cross lines' to which
   Hepner refers are actually very dark blue on a background of pale greenish
   blue.

13 The study score published by Berandol omits many of the Rehearsal numbers. Rehearsal 9 to 14 includes pages 28 to 33. Rehearsal 11–1 to 11+4,
   shown in example 3-8, are found on page 29 of the published score.

14 In his capacity as orchestral player he had already performed a great deal of
   the Romantic symphonic repertoire, and found much of it formally stereotypical. He cites Schumann's symphonies as particularly culpable in this
   respect.

15 Beckwith and Litwack 1992, 498. Presumably the term '12-tone technique' is being used here in its now-accepted sense as an analogue for 'serialism.'

16 As cited in Hepner 1975, 71.

17 Proctor 1980, 74.

18 Freedman contends that these 'eccentric syncopations' are actually derived from East Indian methods of rhythmic construction, and that they become syncopations only when squeezed into a straightforward Western rhythmic context.

19 As cited in Blume and Potvin 1964, 43.

4. The Quest for Independence (1962 to 1969)

1 In this respect he claims also to have been influenced by jazz, in which material is rarely recycled from movement to movement.

2 His arrangements of French-Canadian folk songs in 1950 and 1957 were based on pre-existing music, and his *Two Vocalises* of 1954 were devoid of comprehensible text.

3 Note, too, the metric tension engendered by the hemiola effect in the soprano line, bracketed by measures 5 to 8.

4 For example, see Beckwith and Litwack 1992, 498. In referring to *The Tokaido* the authors remark that 'Freedman's return to 12-tone technique – and his only strict use of it – came in 1964.' Other writers make similar statements about the timing of Freedman's return to serialism.

5 Beckwith and Litwack 1992, 498.

6 That is, one reduces to pc set class 5-19 (01367), two to pc set class 5-6 (01256) and one to pc set class 5-3 (01245).

7 Another interesting insight to be gained from the sketches is that five of the motives are assigned to specific instruments, underlining Freedman's contention that timbre is often one of the first parameters he considers.

8 However, in *The Tokaido* he did exploit the possibilities inherent in the trichordal segmentation of his row, as we shall see.

9 Beckwith and Litwack 1992, 498.

10 The John Adaskin Project was a plan to promote the increased use of Canadian music in the musical education of Canadians.

11 Freedman says that he would particularly like to hear the effect of the 'large walls of sound,' and of the interplay between open and closed mouth sounds.

12 The instrumentation includes timpani, bongos, snare drum, tenor drum, bass drum, suspended cymbals, finger cymbals, triangle, bells, tambourine, and castanets.

13 This was to be the first of many collaborations between Freedman and Macdonald.

14 After the first performance, a number of critics commented somewhat disparagingly on the obvious similarity between this story and that of the ballet *Giselle*, implying that imitation and lack of originality were to be expected in Canadian creative efforts. They apparently did not know that the story on which *Rose Latulippe* was based was published in Quebec three years before *Giselle*'s première in Europe.

15 From a purely practical standpoint, Freedman contends that strict serial composition takes a great deal of time – time that he did not have during the composition of *Rose Latulippe*.

16 Proctor 1980, 137.

17 There are, however, certain inherent characteristics of the row which undeniably exist, though Freedman exploits very few of them, other than the use of invariant dyads as a means of seamless overlap between one row form and another. While the outer trichords are not equivalent, the middle two trichords are, as are the boundary tetrachords, a property which he does not use to mutate from one version of the row to another.

18 The first half of this number series can be discerned as the basis of the rhythmic organization of the 'Dance of the Adolescents' in Stravinsky's *Rite of Spring*. However, Stravinsky told Freedman during the intermission of a recording session at Massey Hall that he was unaware of East Indian rhythmic constructions at the time he wrote the *Rite*.

19 For example, the articles on Freedman in *Contemporary Canadian Composers* and the *Encyclopedia of Music in Canada* make this statement. However, it is possible that the authors were not using the adjective 'twelve-tone' synonymously with 'serial.'

20 Proctor 1980, 154.

21 Freedman maintains that he fully intended the section to exemplify rock and roll, and that the childhood taunt is introduced as a snide comment on the childish, elementary nature of rock, the music most of these musicians grew up with.

22 When Freedman was asked why he did not use a numeric series to create the pitch class row, he replied that he didn't like the musical result. In his words, 'the application of number to pitch confutes the instinct.' Nevertheless, he did make a determined effort to do so in the ballet *Five over Thirteen*, though he eventually discarded the results as being innately unmusical.

23 The other ballets were *Rose Latulippe*, *The Shining People of Leonard Cohen*, *Several Occasions* (set to the music of *Tapestry*), *Romeo and Juliet*, *Reed Song*

(set to the music of *Chalumeau*), and *Breaks* (set to atonal variations on the slow movement of Mozart's *Duo in B^b* for *Violin and Viola*.

24 Both 5 and 13 are part of the summation series 1, 1, 2, 3, 5, 8, 13, 21 ...

25 This is not the first time Freedman has used motives to generate a tone row, as we have seen in the earlier discussion of *Tokaido*, though it is the first time he has used them in precisely this way.

26 The row forms with which motives in the second version are associated are as follows: motive 1: pcs 8 3 9, segment of P0; motive 2: pcs 7 5 2 8, segment of P7; motive 3: 10 1 4, segment of P11 or RI11; motive 4/5: 1 8 / 2 5, segment of P5; motive 6: 1 6 0, segment of I5; motive 7: 10 7 4 6 0 3, segment of RP5; motive 8: 3 4 1, segment of RP11; motive 9: 9 7 5 6, segment of RP1; motive 10: 0 9 11, segment of I5; motive 11: 8 11 1 10, segment of RP1; motive 12: 6 4 7, segment of P5 or RI0.

27 In fact, when Freedman later rescored *Anerca* for piano, harp, and vibraphone he used conventional bar lines to make it easier to conduct.

5. New Directions (1970 to 1976)

1 Freedman later discovered that the bore of the instrument had shrunk, probably because of insufficiently seasoned grenadilla wood. Ironically, a few turns of a specially designed reamer file solved all of his intonation problems.

2 The instruments are bass guitar (bottom stave) and an assortment of percussion instruments in the upper staves. Freedman's directions in the score state that 'the improvisations in the percussion section should be played on instruments that can produce soft, metallic sounds – e.g. cymbals, finger cymbals, bell trees, triangle, etc. – struck by various kinds of clappers. Each player should have as wide a variety of instruments as possible.'

3 As has been mentioned, Freedman attributes his fascination with native peoples to his early childhood memories in Medicine Hat. He remembers being mesmerized by the Indians as he watched them trading their furs at his father's store.

4 Gordon V. Thompson Ltd., 1972.

5 These include temple bells, glass wind chimes, claves, antique cymbals, finger cymbals, vibraphone, xylophone, chimes, glockenspiel, suspended cymbal, gong, timpani, and harp.

6 For further examples see Rehearsals 34, 37, and 43, claves.

7 Max Picard, *The World of Silence*, translated by Stanley Godman (Chicago: H. Regner, 1964).

8 The notes Freedman normally creates prior to embarking on his compositions abound with dramatic imagery, frequently suggesting distinct and
strongly contrasting personalities for his principal thematic materials.

9 In the earliest version of the score Freedman did not require scordatura tuning until partway through the piece, but evidently this created a problem
for the players, so the composer revised the score to specify scordatura tuning from the outset. Despite this concession, the work was largely shunned
by players, who apparently were reluctant to retune their instruments in
this fashion. For this reason, Freedman has withdrawn *Graphic II* from his
repertoire. However, he has recycled some of the material, now using conventional tuning, in his *Graphic VIII.* He also intends to use much of the
remaining material in a string quartet for which he has recently received a
commission.

10 Christianne Sawruk, 'Continuity in Messiaen's "Par lui tout a été fait,"' MA
thesis, University of Western Ontario, 1993.

11 As cited in Shapiro and Cohen 1978, 23 and 54.

12 Sound masses, though present on occasion, are not used as substitutes for
motives in generating coherence. Instead, they function merely as accompaniment to melodic material.

13 For example, in his *Trio for Two Oboes and English Horn* (1948) he had
included a quotation from Debussy's *Nocturnes,* and in *Klee Wyck* (1970) he
had incorporated some authentic Indian songs.

14 This is Freedman's first experiment with polytonality since *Scales in Polytonality,* a pedagogical work written in 1966.

15 In fact, in 1970 he had won the Etrog award (now called the Genie award)
for the best musical score for a feature film. The music was a cantata, *The
Flame Within,* written for the Paul Almond/Genevieve Bujold film, *Act of
the Heart.*

6. The Mature Stylistic Spectrum (1977 to the Present)

1 The origins, specifications, and applications of these scales will be dealt
with later in this chapter.

2 Some sources restrict the term 'third stream' to the combination of 'progres-
sive jazz' with the classical tradition, as seen in the work of Gunther
Schuller in the 1960s. See, for example, the article on jazz in the *Harvard
Dictionary of Music*, ed. Willi Apel, 2nd edition (Belknap Press, 1972).

3 Other such works include *Impromptus* (1980), *Passacaglia for Jazz Band and
Orchestra* (1984), and *Sonata for Symphonic Winds* (1988).

4 The saxophone is joined toward the end of the section by the trombone in a

delicate and intricate duet punctuated by occasional pizzicato comments in the basses.

5 Freedman admits that the inspiration for the humour in *Caper* was indeed the striking contrast between the short bodily stature of Dennis Miller and the immense size of his cumbersome instrument. Freedman wonders whether Miller sensed that this was the case, hence his refusal to play the piece.

6 Another work from this period that is similar in this respect is *Chalumeau* (1981). My discussion of motivic associations in *Chalumeau* can be found in 'Cellular Metamorphosis and Structural Compartmentalization in Harry Freedman's *Chalumeau*,' *Studies in Music* 6 (1981), 48–76.

7 Presumably he discarded his first idea.

8 Robert Cogan, *Sonic Design* (Englewood Cliffs, NJ: Prentice-Hall, 1976).

9 The second movement features rapidly changing metres in one place (Rehearsal 32), and the associated melodic patterning does make a downbeat audible, if irregular. Otherwise this movement is as non-pulsatile as the other two.

10 Freedman frequently uses the term 'Hindu rhythms' in his sketches as a kind of shorthand for the longer term 'East Indian rhythms.'

11 Note the resemblance of Freedman's eight-tone scale (a form of pc set class 8-27) to the octatonic scale (pc set class 8-28) that was an important component in a number of earlier works. The two collections differ only by reversal of one ic pairing.

12 Using Freedman's preferred starting point, this eight-tone scale begins on pc 3 and comprises pcs 3, 5, 7, 8, 9, 11, 0, 2. The seventh element is therefore pc 0.

7. Conclusion

1 One example of a logical process that produces an irregular, unexpected result is the interweaving of two logical number series to form a third, much less predictable series, as described above.

2 Blume and Potvin 1964, 42.

3 The notes for his *Alice in Wonderland* offer an apt illustration. On page 27 he comments: 'Take out these 2 bars if section is too long.'

4 The interview took place in the composer's home on 16 May 2003.

List of Works by Harry Freedman

This list is offered in chronological rather than alphabetical order to conform with the order of presentation used in the book. The date under which each work is listed refers to its year of composition. Detailed information about instrumentation, duration, first performances, and sound recordings is readily available on the Canadian Music Centre website.

1947

Divertimento for Oboe and Strings, CMC ms

1948

Symphonic Suite (for orchestra)

Trio for Two Oboes and English Horn (Variations on 'Poor Wayfarin' Stranger')

1949

Five Pieces for String Quartet, CMC ms

Nocturne I (for orchestra), CMC ms

1950

Six French Canadian Folk Songs (arranged for violin and piano)

1951

'Caricature' (for small orchestra) (second movement of *Matinée Suite*, commissioned by John Adaskin for the CBC radio program 'Opportunity Knocks'), CMC ms

Spiritual; March; Pastorale (for woodwinds)

Suite for Piano, CMC ms

1952

'March for Small Types' (for small orchestra) (first movement of *Matinée Suite*, commissioned by John Adaskin for the CBC radio program 'Opportunity Knocks'), CMC ms

Tableau (for string orchestra, commissioned by the Forest Hill Community Centre Orchestra) Markham, Ontario: Ricordi (Canada), 1960

1954

Two Vocalises (for soprano, clarinet, and piano, commissioned by Avrahm Galper), CMC ms

1955

Fantasia and Dance (for violin and orchestra, commissioned by Jacob Groob) (revised 1959), CMC ms

'Harlem Hoedown' (for small orchestra) (third movement of *Matinée Suite*, commissioned by John Adaskin for the CBC radio program 'Opportunity Knocks'), CMC ms

Scherzo (for piano) (Number 14 in *Fourteen Piano Pieces by Canadian Composers*) Oakville, Ontario: Frederick Harris, 1955

1956

Shadow of the City (incidental music for TV documentary, John Hirsch)

1957

The Bloody Brood (jazz score for feature film, Julian Roffman)

Laurentian Moods (for high school band) (arrangement of French-Canadian folk songs commissioned by W.A. Fisher for the Barrie Collegiate Band)

1958

The Doukhobors (incidental music for TV documentary, Doug Leiterman)

Images (for string orchestra, commissioned by Alexander Brott for the McGill Chamber Society Orchestra through the Lapitsky Foundation of Montreal) (rescored for full orchestra 1953) Mississauga, Ontario: Berandol, 1960

1959

Election! (music for TV documentary, CBC, Doug Leiterman)

India (music for TV documentary, CBC, Ross McLean)

Kingston Pen (music for TV documentary, CBC, Patrick Watson)

United Nations (music for TV documentary, CBC, Doug Leiterman)

Where Will They Go? (music for TV documentary, CBC-Intertel, Patrick Watson)

1960

Symphony no. 1 (for orchestra, commissioned through the Canada Council), CMC ms

1961

The Canvas Barricade (incidental music for the first Canadian play produced at the Stratford Festival)

Micheline (music for TV documentary on Micheline Beauchemin, CBC, Vincent Tovell)

1962

Fantasy and Allegro (for string orchestra, commissioned for the Hart House Orchestra through the Canada Council by the Brantford Musical Society for its sixtieth anniversary), CMC ms

Quintette (for winds) Toronto, Ontario: E.C. Kerby, 1972

Trois poèmes de Jacques Prévert (for soprano and strings or soprano and piano, also exists as *Voice Lines,* a wordless vocalise with either piano or strings, commissioned by Ilona Kombrick through the Canada Council) (revised 1981) CMC ms

20 Million Shoes (music for TV documentary, CBC-Intertel, Doug Leiterman and Beryl Fox)

1963

Bits 'n' Pieces (musical satire, CBC radio, John Reeves)

The Dark Did Not Conquer (music for CBC-TV documentary, Paul Almond)

Pale Horse, Pale Rider (music for TV drama, CBC, Eric Till)

This Hour Has Seven Days (music for CBC-TV public affairs series, Patrick Watson and Doug Leiterman)

1964

Chaconne (for orchestra, commissioned by the CBC music department for CBC Symphony Orchestra broadcasts) (revised 1981), CMC ms

Journey to the Centre (music for CBC-TV documentary, Paul Almond)

Spring Song (incidental music to CBC-TV drama, Paul Almond)

Three Vocalises (for chorus, commissioned by the Canadian Music Centre for the first John Adaskin Project) Toronto, Ontario: Leeds (Canada), 1965

The Tokaido (for mixed choir and woodwind quintet, commissioned by the Festival Singers of Toronto), CMC ms

The Voyage of Sinbad (music for CBC radio drama, Digby Peers)

1965

Let Me Count the Ways (music for CBC-TV drama, Paul Almond; also exists as a suite for chamber orchestra)

Romeo and Jeanette (music for CBC-TV drama, Paul Almond)

700 Million (incidental music for CBC-TV documentary on China, Patrick Watson)

Three Duets (for basses and cellos, written for Fred Zimmerman)

Totem and Taboo (for chorus and piano solo, commissioned by the Festival Singers of Toronto)

Trio (for basses or cellos, written for Fred Zimmerman)

Variations (for flute, oboe, and harpsichord, commissioned by the CBC for the Baroque Trio of Montreal), CMC ms

Vincent Massey: A Portrait (music for CBC-TV documentary, Vincent Tovell)

1966

Anerca (for soprano and piano, commissioned by Lois Marshall with the collaboration of the Canadian Music Centre through a grant from the Canadian

Centennial Commission) (revised for soprano, vibraphone, harp, and piano in 1992), CMC ms

China: The Roots of Madness (music for CBS-Wolper Productions)

A Little Symphony (for orchestra, commissioned by the Saskatoon Symphony Orchestra through the Canadian Centennial Commission), CMC ms

The Mills of the Gods (music for CBC-TV documentary on Vietnam with live footage, Beryl Fox)

Rose Latulippe (full-length ballet in three acts by Brian Macdonald, also exists as a suite for orchestra, commissioned by the Royal Winnipeg Ballet through the Canadian Centennial Commission) (revised 1976), CMC ms

Scales in Polytonality (études for school ensembles), CMC ms

1967

Armana (for orchestra, commissioned by the Canadian Broadcasting Corporation), CMC ms

Isabel (music for feature film with Geneviève Bujold, Paul Almond)

October Beach (music for CBC-TV documentary, Paul Almond)

Sir Tony (music for CBC-TV documentary on Sir Tyrone Guthrie, Ross McLean)

Tangents (for orchestra, commissioned by the National Youth Orchestra Association of Canada through the Canadian Centennial Commission), CMC ms

1968

The Flame Within (for chorus and organ, cantata for feature film *Act of the Heart*) Toronto, Ontario: Leeds (Canada), 1968

Poems of Young People (for low voice and piano, commissioned by the CBC for Maureen Forrester), CMC ms

Sicilienne (for piano) CMC ms

Toccata (for soprano and flute, written for Robert Aitken and Mary Morrison) Toronto, Ontario: E.C. Kerby, 1972

Treadmill (music for CBC-TV documentary, Ross McLean)

1969

Five over Thirteen (ballet by Brian Macdonald, commissioned by the Royal Winnipeg Ballet)

Joey II (music for film documentary, National Film Board, Ross McLean)

Ookpik (for choir, words by Dennis Lee) Toronto, Ontario: Anerca Music, 1983 (withdrawn by the composer)

1970

A la claire fontaine (folk song arrangement for band), CMC ms

Blanche comme la neige (folk song arrangement for band), CMC ms

Echo Prelude (for band), CMC ms

Etude (for band), CMC ms

Four Pieces for School Band

Klee Wyck (for orchestra, inspired by paintings of Emily Carr, commissioned by the Victoria Symphony Orchestra through the Canada Council on the occasion of British Columbia's centennial celebrations) (revised 1986), CMC ms

March? (for orchestra, commissioned by the Junior Women's Committee of the Toronto Symphony for young audiences), CMC ms

Night (music for CBC-TV drama)

November (music for National Film Board production)

Scenario (for alto saxophone, bass guitar, and orchestra, commissioned by the CBC), CMC ms

The Shining People of Leonard Cohen (ballet by Brian Macdonald to poetry of Leonard Cohen, commissioned by the Royal Winnipeg Ballet)

Soliloquy (for flute and piano), Toronto, Ontario: Leeds, 1972

1971

Graphic I (for orchestra and tape, composed for the fiftieth anniversary of the Toronto Symphony), CMC ms

Keewaydin (for SSA choir, commissioned by William and Barbara Heintzman for the Bishop Strachan School Choir), Toronto, Ontario: Gordon V. Thompson, 1972; (rescored for SATB choir), Toronto, Ontario: Anerca Music, 1985

Much Ado about Nothing (incidental music, Stratford Festival)

Preludes (for orchestra; orchestration of ten of Debussy's *Preludes for Piano*, Book 1, commissioned by the CBC)

Short Pieces for Children's Concerts (composed for various groups in the Toronto Symphony)

Tikki Tikki Tembo (for narrator and woodwind quintet, commissioned by the Dundas Public Library Board), CMC ms

1972

As You Like It (incidental music, Stratford Festival, William Hutt)

August (for French horn ensemble) (revised 1981)

Captives of the Faceless Drummer (incidental music, Lennoxville Festival, George Ryga, directed by William Davis)

Graphic II (for string quartet, commissioned by the Courtenay Youth Music Centre for the Purcell String Quartet through the Canada Council) (withdrawn by the composer August 1992), CMC ms

Pan (for soprano, flute, and piano, commissioned by the CBC for the Lyric Arts Trio), CMC ms

'TILT' (music for animation documentary, National Film Board)

Twelfth Night (incidental music, Toronto Arts Productions, Leon Major)

1973

Bells of Hell (music for CBC-TV, George Jonas)

Lines (for clarinet solo, commissioned by Ronald de Kant) (revised 1974), London, Ontario: Jaymar, 1991

Little Acorns (short pieces for school band, school music project begun in 1970, eventually to have been three volumes of contemporary pieces, from elementary to advanced), CMC ms

The Pyx (music for feature film, Harvey Hart)

Quartet (for trombones, cellos, or bassoons, composed for the Courtenay Youth Music Centre ensembles), CMC ms

Romeo and Juliet (ballet by Brian Macdonald for Renaissance consort, originally entitled *Star-Cross'd*) (revised and augmented with additional music, 1975)

Sunlight on Sarah (incidental music for George Ryga play directed by William Davis, Festival Lennoxville)

Tapestry (for orchestra; also used in *Several Occasions*, ballet by Brian Macdonald, commissioned by the National Arts Centre Orchestra), CMC ms

1974

Encounter (for violin and piano, commissioned for Steven Staryk by the Courtenay Youth Music Centre through the Canada Council), CMC ms

Psalm 137 (for tenor and organ, commissioned by the CBC, John Reeves)

Songs from Shakespeare (for choir, songs from three Shakespeare productions, *Much Ado about Nothing*, *As You Like It*, and *Twelfth Night*), Toronto, Ontario: Anerca Music, 1974 (reworked in 1990 for four solo voices and two pianos)

1975

Friendship (music for CBC-TV drama, Paul Almond)

Nocturne II (for orchestra, commissioned by the CBC for the Calgary Philharmonic), CMC ms

Twelfth Night (incidental music, Stratford Festival, David Jones)

Two Sonnets of Love and Age (for soprano, baritone, woodwind quintet, and brass quintet, commissioned by the CBC, text by John Reeves), CMC ms

Vignette (for clarinet and piano, written for the Toronto Symphony Dream Auction), CMC ms

1976

Alice in Wonderland (for soprano, alto, baritone, and instrumental ensemble, written for Camerata for puppet presentation, commissioned by Toronto Arts Productions), CMC ms

Celebration (concerto for saxophone and orchestra, commissioned by the CBC on the occasion of Gerry Mulligan's fiftieth birthday) (revised 1980), CMC ms

'1847' (music for TV film, part of Imperial Oil's 'Newcomers' series, produced by Neilson-Ferns, directed by Eric Till)

The Explainer (for flute, oboe, cello, percussion, piano, and narrator/conductor, commissioned by Days Months Years to Come through the Canada Council), CMC ms

Five Rings (for brass quintet, commissioned by the Cultural Committee of the Olympics for the Canadian Brass, through the Canada Council) (revised 1981), CMC ms

Fragments of Alice (for soprano, alto, baritone, and chamber ensemble, commissioned by New Music Concerts), CMC ms

Mono (for solo French horn, commissioned by Robert E. Creech), CMC ms

Pastorale (for choir and solo English horn, commissioned by the music department of the University of Prince Edward Island through the Canada Council), CMC ms

Tsolum Summer (for flute, percussion, and strings, commissioned by the Hamilton Philharmonic Institute through the Canada Council), CMC ms

1978

Blue ... Green ... White ... (for choir, songs of the eastern provinces, commissioned by the Canadian Music Centre through the Ontario Arts Council), Toronto, Ontario: Anerca Music, 1983

Caper (for solo tuba, commissioned by Dennis Miller through the Canada Council), CMC ms

Epitaph for Igor Stravinsky (for tenor, string quartet, and four trombones, commissioned by CBC radio, John Reeves) (revised for tenor and string quartet 1998), CMC ms

Kavik the Wolf Dog (music for TV feature film, NBC–Jon Slan Enterprises)

Monday Gig (for woodwind quintet, commissioned by Contemporary Showcase through the McLean Foundation and the Ontario Arts Council), Toronto, Ontario: Anerca Music, 1981 and London, Ontario: Jaymar, 1992

November (for soprano or mezzo-soprano, flute, vibraphone, and harp, reworking of *November* 1970), CMC ms

Sicilienne (for guitar, revised version of *Sicilienne* 1968, revised and fingered by Robert Feuerstein)

1979

Abracadabra (one-act opera, libretto by Mavor Moore, commissioned by the Courtenay Youth Music Centre), CMC ms

Opus Pocus (for flute, violin, viola, and cello, commissioned by the Galliard Ensemble through the Ontario Arts Council), CMC ms

3 for 2 (for clarinet and alto and soprano saxophones, commissioned by Paul Brodie through the Ontario Arts Council), CMC ms

1980

Blue (for string quartet, commissioned by the Purcell String Quartet through the Canada Council) (revised 1981), CMC ms

Celebration Variation (for brass quintet; one of a number of variations in *Tribute*, written in honour of Louis Applebaum on a theme from Applebaum's *Suite of Miniature Dances*), CMC ms

Impromptus (for mezzo-soprano and guitar, commissioned through the Canada Council by the Guitar Society of Toronto for Guitar '81), CMC ms

Nocturne III (for choir and orchestra, commissioned through the Canada Council by the Bach-Elgar Choral Society of Hamilton for its seventy-fifth anniversary season), CMC ms

Pyramid of Roses (music for film by Chris Chapman on 'Vale Variations' of Harold Town)

1981

Chalumeau (for clarinet and string orchestra or clarinet and string quartet, commissioned by the CBC for James Campbell) (revised 1992), CMC ms

Much Ado about Nothing (for harpsichord and guitar, suite from *Much Ado about Nothing*, 1971), CMC ms

Royal Flush (concerto grosso for brass quintet and orchestra, commissioned by the Montreal Symphony Orchestra through the Canada Council), CMC ms

Something Hidden – A Portrait of Wilder Penfield (music for National Film Board film)

A Spring Song (for choir, reworking of *Spring Song*, 1964), London, Ontario: Jaymar, 1991

1982

Accord (for violin and orchestra, commissioned by the Montreal International Competitions through the Canada Council), CMC ms

And Now It Is Today Oh Yes (for soprano and instrumental ensemble; musical settings of selections from Gertrude Stein's *Everybody's Autobiography*, commissioned by New Music Concerts through the Ontario Arts Council), CMC ms

Concerto for Orchestra (commissioned by the Toronto Symphony through the Canada Council for the orchestra's first season at Roy Thomson Hall) (revisions 1985 and 1990), CMC ms

A Time Is Coming (for choir, commissioned by the CBC for the Elmer Iseler Singers), CMC ms

1983

Alice: 3 Songs and an Egg (for soprano, mezzo-soprano, alto, tenor, baritone, and bass, commissioned by the Tapestry Singers through the Ontario Arts Council), CMC ms

Against Oblivion (music for the Hand and Eye Series, CBC, Katherine Smalley)

All That Glistens (music for the Hand and Eye Series, CBC, Katherine Smalley)

Fanfare for Six Voices (commissioned by the Tapestry Singers)

Oiseaux exotiques (ballet score based on Venezuelan folk music, also exists as a suite for orchestra, commissioned by the National Ballet of Canada) (revised 1985), CMC ms

Passacaglia for Jazz Band and Orchestra (commissioned by CJRT-FM through the Canada Council for the Boss Brass and the CJRT Concert Orchestra for Toronto's sesquicentennial), CMC ms

The Sax Chronicles (for saxophone and orchestra, commissioned by Gerry Mulligan)

Symphony no. 3 (for orchestra, commissioned by the Regina Symphony Orchestra through the Canada Council) (revised 1985), CMC ms

1985

Connections (film score, National Film Board)

Fanfares for Century II (for brass and percussion, commissioned by the Royal Conservatory of Music to commemorate its centennial), CMC ms

A Garland for Terry (for orchestra and narrator; in memory of Terry Fox, narrative by Miriam Waddington, commissioned by the Victoria Symphony Orchestra), CMC ms

Rent-a-Rag (for piano, published in the Royal Conservatory of Music Grade 8 examination book), Oakville, Ontario: Frederick Harris, 1988

1986

Contrasts (The Web and the Wind) (for fifteen solo strings, commissioned by the Chamber Players of Toronto through the Ontario Arts Council and the Canada Council), CMC ms

Encore! Encore! (incidental music for multi-media presentation for Expo 86)

Graphic VI: Town (for orchestra, impressions of four paintings by Harold Town, commissioned by the Windsor Symphony Orchestra through the Ontario Arts Council) (withdrawn by the composer in 1995)

Heroes of Our Time (for orchestra, ballet by Nancy Lima Dent, commissioned by Encore! Encore!), CMC ms

Memento (for piano solo), CMC ms

Rhymes from the Nursery (for treble chorus and flute, commissioned by the Toronto Children's Chorus through the Canada Council), CMC ms

1987

Breaks (for two violins and two violas, variations on Mozart's *Duo in B^b for Violin and Viola* for ballet by Brian Macdonald)

Fragments of Alice (for actors, singers, and dancers, commissioned by the National Film Board; stage presentation of scenes from the two Alice books)

1988

A Dance on the Earth (for orchestra, three dances from Venezuela, America, and

Ghana, commissioned by the Thunder Bay Symphony through the Canada Council and dedicated to Margaret Laurence), CMC ms

Little Girl Blew (for solo bass clarinet or solo B♭ clarinet), CMC ms

Sonata for Symphonic Winds (for wind ensemble, commissioned by the Toronto Symphony Youth Orchestra), CMC ms

1989

Bones (for marimba solo, commissioned by Beverly Johnston through the Ontario Arts Council), CMC ms

Scenes from Alice (stage presentation by Smith and Gilmour of several chapters of the Alice books)

Short Story (for English horn solo, commissioned by Lawrence Cherney) (revised 1990), CMC ms

Touchings (for percussion ensemble and orchestra, commissioned by Nexus through the Canada Council), CMC ms

1991

Another Monday Gig (for jazz ensemble, commissioned by Hemispheres through the Ontario Arts Council), CMC ms

Town (for orchestra, an impression of Harold Town, the man and his art, commissioned by the Esprit Orchestra through the Ontario Arts Council), CMC ms

1992

Downwind (for accordion and bass clarinet, commissioned by Joseph Macerollo through the Ontario Arts Council), CMC ms

Strands of Blue (for chamber ensemble, commissioned by New Music Concerts through the Canada Council), CMC ms (withdrawn by the composer in 1995)

1993

A Bouquet of Florrie (for soprano, clarinet, cello, and keyboards, commissioned by Thira, Winnipeg)

Spirit Song (for soprano and string quartet, commissioned by Music Toronto through the Ontario Arts Council), CMC ms

1994

Indigo (for twenty-two solo strings, commissioned by CBC for the Manitoba Chamber Orchestra), CMC ms

Touchpoints (for flute, viola, and harp, commissioned by Trio Lyra through the Ontario Arts Council), CMC ms

1995

Blow, Blow, Thou Winter Wind (for choir, commissioned through the Canada Council), London, Ontario: Jaymar, 1995

Blue Light (for flute, clarinet/bass clarinet, violin, cello, and piano, commissioned by Aurora Musicale, Winnipeg)

Bright Angels (for soprano and guitar or lute; music for the balcony scene of Shakespeare's *Romeo and Juliet*), CMC ms

Kitchen Cantata (for mezzo-soprano and piano, libretto by Mary Lou Fallis, commissioned by Classical Cabaret through the Toronto Arts Council and the Ontario Arts Council), CMC ms

Saxtet (for saxophone quartet, commissioned by the Selmer Saxophone Quartet through the Canada Council), CMC ms

1996

Higher (for bass clarinet and bass oboe or cello, commissioned by Bass Instincts through the Canada Council), CMC ms

Marigold (for viola, percussion, and synthesizer, commissioned by Rivka Golani with the assistance of the Canada Council)

1997

Borealis (for orchestra, children's choir, and three SATB choirs, commissioned by CBC for the first Northern Encounters Festival), CMC ms

Dances (for solo harp, four pieces based on popular music of the Americas, commissioned by Erica Goodman through the Ontario Arts Council)

1998

Marigold (concerto for viola and orchestra, reworking of *Marigold* 1996)

Voices (for choir, commissioned by Soundstreams through the Ontario Arts Council for the Elmer Iseler Singers and the Stuttgart Chamber Choir), CMC ms

2000

Graphic VIII (for string quartet, written for the Penderecki Quartet, with the assistance of the Canada Council)

Graphic IX (for sixteen solo strings, written for Harry Somers, commissioned by the Royal Canadian Academy of Arts with the assistance of Music Canada Musique 2000), CMC ms

2001

Aqsaqniq (for children's choir and piano, commissioned by the Toronto Children's Chorus through the Ontario Arts Council), CMC ms

Bright Angels (vocalise for soprano and flute, reworking of the balcony scene from *Romeo and Juliet*), CMC ms

Duke (for orchestra, a symphonic tribute to the music of Duke Ellington, with the assistance of the Canada Council)

2002

Romp and Reverie (for solo flute, commissioned by Robert Cram through the Ontario Arts Council), CMC ms

Valleys (for choir, commissioned by Soundstreams through the Canada Council), CMC ms

2003

Phoenix (for string quartet, commissioned by New Music Concerts and the
   Laidlaw Foundation)
Spanish Skies (cycle of five songs to poetry of Marianne Bindig, commissioned
   by Stacie Dunlop with the assistance of the Laidlaw Foundation)
Tribute (symphonic synthesis of music from Harry Somer's opera *Mario and the
   Magician*, commissioned by Barbara Chilcott Somers)

Works Cited

Beckwith, John. 1969. 'About Canadian Music: The P.R. Failure.' *Musicanada* 21 (1969), 4.

Beckwith, John, and Linda Litwack. 1992. 'Freedman, Harry.' In *Encyclopedia of Music in Canada*, ed. Helmut Kallmann, Gilles Potvin, and Kenneth Winters. Toronto: University of Toronto Press, 498–500.

Blume, Helmut, and Gilles Potvin. 1964. *Thirty-Four Biographies of Canadian Composers*. Montreal: Canadian Broadcasting Corporation, 42–5.

Hepner, Lee. 1975. 'Freedman, Harry.' In *Contemporary Canadian Composers*, ed. Keith MacMillan and John Beckwith. Toronto, London, New York: Oxford University Press (Canada), 71–5.

Keillor, Elaine. 1994. *John Weinzweig and His Music: The Radical Romantic of Canada*. Composers of North America series, no. 15. Metuchen, New Jersey, and London: Scarecrow Press.

Proctor, George. 1980. *Canadian Music of the Twentieth Century*. Toronto, Buffalo, London: University of Toronto Press.

Shapiro, David and Arthur Cohen. 1978. *The New Art of Colour: The Writings of Robert and Sonia Delaunay*. New York: Viking Press, 23 and 54.

Selective Bibliography

Beckwith, John. 'Composers in Toronto and Montreal.' *University of Toronto Quarterly* 26: 1 (1956): 47–69.
– 'What Every U.S. Musician Should Know about Contemporary Canadian Music.' *Musicanada* 29 (1970): 5–7, 12–13, 18.
Beckwith, John, and Udo Kasemets. *The Modern Composer and His World.* Toronto: University of Toronto Press, 1961.
Beckwith, John, and Linda Litwack. 'Freedman, Harry.' In *Encyclopedia of Music in Canada*, ed. Helmut Kallmann, Gilles Potvin, and Kenneth Winters. Toronto: University of Toronto Press, 1992, 498–500.
Blume, Helmut, and Gilles Potvin. *Thirty-Four Biographies of Canadian Composers.* Montreal: Canadian Broadcasting Corporation, 1964, 42–45.
Boothroyd, David A. 'Pentland, Freedman and Prévost: Three Canadian String Quartets, 1968 to 1972.' MA Thesis, University of Western Ontario, 1979.
Bradley, Ian L. *Twentieth Century Canadian Composers.* Vol. 1. Agincourt, Ont.: GLC Publishers, 1977, 139–67.
Desautels, Andrée. 'The History of Canadian Composition 1610–1967.' In *Aspects of Music in Canada*, ed. Arnold Walter. Toronto: University of Toronto Press, 1969, 90–142.
Dixon, Gail. 'Harry Freedman: A Survey.' *Studies in Music* 5 (1980): 122–44.
– 'Cellular Metamorphosis and Structural Compartmentalization in Harry Freedman's *Chalumeau.*' *Studies in Music* 6 (1981): 48–76.
– 'A Composer Takes Stock.' *Canadian Composer* 176 (1982): 4–7, 33.
– 'Harry Freedman's Sketchbooks.' *Canadian Composer* 177 (1983): 16–21.
– 'Freedman, Harry." In *The New Groves Dictionary of Music and Musicians*, Vol. 9, ed. Stanley Sadie, exec. ed. John Tyrell. Toronto: University of Toronto Press, 2001, 220–2.
Hepner, Lee. 'An Analytical Study of Selected Canadian Orchestral Composi-

tions at the Mid-Twentieth-Century.' PhD diss., New York University School of Education, 1971.

– 'Freedman, Harry.' In *Contemporary Canadian Composers*, ed. Keith MacMillan and John Beckwith. Toronto, London, New York: Oxford University Press (Canada), 1975, 71–5.

McGee, Timothy J. *The Music of Canada*. Toronto, London: W.W. Norton, 1985, 114, 124, 126–7.

Napier, Ronald. *A Guide to Canada's Composers*. Willowdale, Ont.: Avondale Press, 1976.

Nichols, Kenneth. 'The Orchestral Compositions of Harry Freedman: A Parametric Analysis of Major Works Written between 1952–67.' PhD diss., University of Minnesota, 1981.

Proctor, George. *Canadian Music of the Twentieth Century*. Toronto, Buffalo, London: University of Toronto Press, 1980.

Slonimsky, Nicolas. *Baker's Biographical Dictionary of Musicians*. New York: Schirmer, 1992.

Wilkinson, Bryan. 'Harry Freedman: An Exciting Composer.' *Canadian Composer* 17 (1967): 4–5, 36–7, 46.

Index